D1155061

The Land of the Five Flavors

ARTS AND TRADITIONS OF THE TABLE

民以食爲天

庚寅春賀林書

The Land of the Five Flavors

A CULTURAL HISTORY OF CHINESE CUISINE

Thomas O. Höllmann

Translated by Karen Margolis

COLUMBIA UNIVERSITY PRESS   NEW YORK

Columbia University·Press
Publishers Since 1893
New York   Chichester, West Sussex
Copyright © 2010 Verlag C. H. Beck oHG, Munich
Translation copyright © 2014 Columbia University Press
All rights reserved
Support for this translation was funded in part by Breuninger Foundation and the Department of Asian Studies, Ludwig Maximilian University of Munich.

Library of Congress Cataloging-in-Publication Data

Höllmann, Thomas O.
   [Schlafender Lotos, trunkenes Huhn. English]
   The land of the five flavors : a cultural history of chinese cuisine / Thomas O.
Höllmann; translated by Karen Margolis.
       pages cm. — (Arts and traditions of the table. Perspectives on culinary history)
   German subtitle: Kulturgeschichte der chinesischen Küche
   Text in English, translated from German.
   Includes bibliographical references and index.
   ISBN 978-0-231-16186-2 (cloth : alk. paper) — ISBN 978-0-231-53654-7 (ebook)
   1. Cooking, Chinese.   2. China—Social life and customs.   I. Title.   II. Title:
Kulturgeschichte der chinesischen Küche.   III. Title: Cultural history of chinese
cuisine.
   TX724.5.C5H64713 2013
   641.5951—dc23
                                                                    2013016126

c 10 9 8 7 6 5 4 3 2 1

COVER IMAGE: Marriage Feast, nineteenth-century Chinese painting. Victoria and Albert
Museum, London. Eileen Tweedy/The Art Archive at Art Resource, NY

COVER DESIGN: Milenda Nan Ok Lee
FRONTISPIECE: Calligraphy by He Lin (2010)

References to Internet Web sites (URLs) were accurate at the time of writing. Neither the
author nor Columbia University Press is responsible for URLs that may have expired or
changed since the manuscript was prepared.

Contents

Preface

"To the people, food is heaven." This is the meaning of the calligraphy by He Lin that forms the frontispiece of this book. The proverb originates from a historical work compiled in the second century (*Hanshu*, chapter 43). Today it is usually associated with epicurean pleasure, but this is not exactly what the saying originally meant. The "heaven" referred to here was not seen as a kind of ideal paradise but as a supreme force. In other words, for the majority of people living in China at that time, nothing was more important than having enough to eat.

A serious history of food culture should offer more than a chronicle of epicurean indulgence and should go beyond examining the social framework of nutrition. It should focus both on extravagance and the impact of hunger and austerity. It should also retrace traditions dating back several thousand years and indicate trends that have only recently come to light.

From a long-term perspective it seems quite clear that at least until the globalization thrust that swept China around the dawn of the third millennium, continuity was stronger than change. I have therefore chosen to explore the different topics systematically instead of using a chronological structure; I have given examples rather than following a continuous narrative thread; and I have tried to tell stories rather than simply presenting facts.

I hope this book succeeds in showing how the paradigm of nutrition in China opens a window on wider historical relationships and offers an attractive approach to Chinese history for readers who may have had little interest in East Asia so far. That—aside from the joy of cooking and spinning tales—is what really motivated me to explore this theme.

Many things that seem broadly homogenous reveal surprising regional and social differences on closer inspection. Nonetheless, generalizations can sometimes be legitimate. Ultimately, there are always some kinds of exceptions, and it would make no sense to focus on every anomaly.

This book includes recipes to give readers a genuine flavor of Chinese cooking, but it is not designed as a cookbook. Keeping the balance between authenticity and feasibility requires all kinds of compromises. Whereas beginners may sometimes feel overwhelmed, experienced cooks will find some of the instructions superfluous and may frown on certain simplifications. It is difficult to avoid concessions, even in the choice of terms. To give just one example, "rice wine" is repeatedly mentioned as an ingredient, although from a scientific perspective it is clearly a type of beer because it is a grain product. But correct terminology is one thing, and successful shopping quite another.

China is a culinary cosmos that requires a classifying structure. For around the past two thousand years, the five flavors (sour, bitter, sweet, pungent, and salty) have been accepted as a general framework. This classification derives from the five phases (wood, fire, earth, metal, water), a schema that may seem quite rigid but that actually bears far more relation to reality than similar ancient notions such as the five points of the compass or the five seasons.

Over the centuries the culinary arts and banqueting have given rise to a rich literary tradition. To convey something of the atmosphere of these writings I have interspersed the narrative with citations, mostly originating from primary Chinese sources. Readers looking for further inspiration will surely find something to their taste in the comprehensive bibliography. I can also recommend a delightful cinematic variation on the theme: *Eat Drink Man Woman* (*Yin shi nan nü*), a tender, ironic movie by Taiwanese director Ang Lee that counterpoints a story of family quarrels with exquisite scenes of culinary brilliance.

Many people have contributed to producing this book. I would particularly like to thank Chen Ganglin, Oliver Dauberschmidt, Rebecca Ehrenwirth, Waltraud Gerstendörfer, Sabine Höllmann, Shung Müller, Marc Nürnberger, Armin Selbitschka, Armin Sorge, Sandra Sukrow, and Christiane Tholen for reading the manuscript critically; Christiane Zeile and Heiko Hortsch from the publisher C.H. Beck, who were responsible for the original German edition; Jiang Bo, Hans van Ess,

Jasmin Föll, Jin Tao, Bruno Richtsfeld, and Zhu Qingsheng for their valuable suggestions; and He Lin for the calligraphy. For this English language edition I would like to express my gratitude to the editor, Jennifer Crewe, and her team at Columbia University Press, and especially to Karen Margolis for her excellent translation.

Translator's note: I would like to thank Caroline Bynum and Karine Chemla for their invaluable help and advice in preparing this edition.

The Land of the Five Flavors

Chapter One

Rice Doesn't Rain from Heaven

Prestige and Consumption

"If there is anything we [the Chinese] are serious about, it is not religion or learning, but food." In the 1930s, the Chinese writer Lin Yutang summed up the culinary aspirations of his fellow countrymen and women as a common denominator in his book *My Country and My People* (p. 337). He may have exaggerated, but a cultivated approach to food certainly plays a bigger role as a constitutive element of culture in China than in other parts of the world. It is probably no coincidence that some important statesmen in antiquity are said to have started out as butchers or cooks. Then again, mastery of the culinary profession could be risky, and some chefs ended up being obliged to accompany their lords to the grave— to be buried along with the well-stocked pantry.

Of course, the degree of hedonism varied through the ages. Although there were times when corpulence could be interpreted as a sign of social status, in other periods austerity was definitely indicated. Women, above all, were subject to the dictates of fashion. The transformation in the ideal of beauty under the Tang dynasty, which occurred in two successive stages, is particularly striking. Tight-fitting garments accentuated the desirable slim figure of the early period, whereas a full figure and loose robes were fashionable in

> The government of a kingdom [basically follows the same principles] as the preparation of small sea animals.
>
> *Laozi* (6th century B.C.), chapter 60
>
> "Excellent," the prince said . . . , "I have heard the words of my butcher, and learned from them the nourishment of (our) life."
>
> *Zhuangzi* (around 300 B.C.), chapter 3

the late period. This is usually explained with reference to Yang Guifei (719–756), a buxom concubine of the emperor's, but clay sculptures excavated from graves show that this development must have begun much earlier.

Admittedly, the historical sources mostly reveal information about the life of the upper class. They show a sovereign at the pinnacle of society who saw himself as the mediator between different worlds and derived his legitimation from a mandate bestowed on him by heaven, at least temporarily. In time, the absolutist claim of the kings—and later the emperors—became limited by a wide range of regulations governing the proper execution of official business. Many rituals that contributed to setting social norms were connected with the intake of food. In other words, eating offered more than sheer pleasure, even if the *Lüshi chunqiu* (chapter 14) remarked as early as the third century B.C., "Only if one is chosen as the Son of Heaven will the tastiest delicacies be prepared [for him]."

The connection with the state cult is also evident in works devoted to custom and etiquette, including the *Zhouli* (especially chapters 4–6), compiled at the beginning of the first century B.C. Its idealized survey of the past reports that at one time more than half of the total royal household of nearly 4,000 was occupied with preparing and serving food and drink. However, it is not easy to distinguish between the rather profane tasks of providing the ruler with food and comfort, and the work related to regular duties in offering sacrifices.

Overlaps in these spheres of activity also occurred in later epochs. Still, in the year 1435 around 5,000 kitchen staff were said to have been exclusively engaged in catering for the emperor's personal sustenance and the banquets he gave. In the following century the figure seems to have risen to as many as 8,000 servants, until falling back to nearly its old level toward the end of the Ming dynasty. The finer the porcelain, the more careful the lackeys had to be; for large receptions there was a stock of tableware numbering more than 300,000 individual pieces. Even beyond grand events, substantial fare had to be dished up. For instance, two years before the end of the Qing dynasty, 2,360 kilograms of meat, 164 ducks, and 274 chickens were available every month just for meals for the emperor Xuantong (reigned 1908–1911), who was then four years old, and the five highest-ranking ladies at court.

It is impossible to retrace how much the servants profited from this gluttony; but we can assume that everything left over from the meals—

MONTHLY ALLOCATIONS OF MEAT AND FOWL FOR THE EMPEROR'S CLOSEST
CIRCLE IN THE YEAR 1909.

	Meat jin	Duck jin	Chickens Quantity
Emperor Xuantong	810	90	150
Longyu, Emperor Guangxu's widow	1860	30	80
2 "widow" concubines, 1st rank, each	360	15	15
2 "widow" concubines, 2nd rank, each	285	7	7

Based on the descriptions of the Last Emperor in *Wode qianban shenghuo* (1964), p. 52. At that time, one *jin* was
roughly equivalent to 597g.

and that was the lion's share—found a taker somewhere. What we do know is that there were separate food supplies for members of the court, who included Crown Councilors, officers of the Imperial Guard and representatives of the academy, and the eunuchs. None of them went hungry either, because monthly household expenditure amounted to nearly 15,000 ounces of silver. However, this "basic provision" did not include expenditures on drinks, fruit, and sweets, nor did it factor in the special expenses that could lead to doubling or trebling costs.

> At a sign, the poor stood up in an orderly fashion: the men on one side, the women on the other. The line had to pass by a narrow point at which each person received a helping of rice and herbs and brought [the food] to an assigned place. . . . As soon as the dishes were empty they were collected and washed; then it was the turn of the next [group of] needy people.
>
> Letter of August 20, 1704, from the Jesuit priest Pierre Jartoux (Jartoux 1714, p. 213)

By comparison, the soup kitchens for the poor that opened in Beijing during the winter every year from 1652 onward each received a monthly supply of nearly 4.3 metric tons of grain, the main soup ingredient. This was enough to produce around 60,000 portions and cost just about 200 ounces of silver—not much, considering the high priority placed on appeasing hunger at court.

Above all, efficient management of disasters was crucial for the emperor personally, because man-made and natural crises—like omens of ill fortune—could be interpreted as symptoms that he was losing his legitimacy. In fact, there were times when history resembled a succession of debacles. Under the Han dynasty alone more than 200 transregional famines were caused by drought, floods, cold snaps, storms, earthquakes, and insect plagues—not to mention food shortages due to wars, riots, and ruthless pursuit of profit.

In that situation, full public granaries were a guarantee of stability and continuity. One consequence was that under the Tang dynasty any public officials or supervisors who allowed stored food to rot by neglecting ventilation of the buildings faced penalties of up to three years' forced labor. Yet even draconian sentences could not prevent famine. It was far more important to evolve long-term strategies for creating adequate reserves, both to prevent private speculation in seeds and grain and to secure adequate provision in emergencies.

> Agriculture is the foundation of the world. As to real gold, pearls, or jade, when one is hungry, they cannot be eaten; when one is cold, they cannot be worn [to protect against the weather].
>
> Edict from the year 141 B.C., cited in *Hanshu* (115), chapter 5. (*The Annals of Emperor Hsiao-Ching*.)

Archaeological finds in Baizhuang (Huayin district) give an idea of the huge size of agricultural buildings, which were mostly used to store grain. Between 1980 and 1983, parts of a building complex were uncovered on the excavation site around 130 kilometers east of Xi'an. An inscription on an eaves tile described it as a "granary for the capital." The area, surrounded by a massive embankment, covered nearly 800,000 square meters altogether; the biggest building, which was more than 60 meters long, must have been very impressive. Coin finds and references in historiographical texts indicate that the complex was built in the reign of Emperor Wu (140–87 B.C.) of the Han dynasty.

Eating outdoors (around 1900)

Many of the granaries were multistoried, and some were actually built as towers. This is shown mainly by innumerable finds of clay miniatures deposited in graves. Sometimes they depict people measuring grain in front of the building. Most Chinese historians relate these images to the oppressive tax collection system, which is understandable because taxes in the Chinese imperial period often had to be paid in the form of cereals. Conversely, social norms obliged landlords to distribute seeds and grain to the population in times of need. While bearing in mind that the pictorial agendas in tombs were generally intended to honor the entombed person posthumously, this strongly suggests that, regardless of the

THE DYNASTIES (OVERVIEW)

Xia		21st century–16th century B.C.	
Shang		16th century–11th century B.C.	
Zhou	Western Zhou	11th century–771 B.C.	
	Eastern Zhou	771–221 B.C.	
Qin		221–207 B.C.	
Han	Early Han	207 B.C.–9 A.D.	9–23 Wang Mang
	Late Han	24–220	Interregnum: Xin
Three Kingdoms	Wei	220–265	
	Shu	221–263	
	Wu	222–280	
	Jin	Early Jin	265–316
			304–439 Foreign dynasties in the north
	Late Jin	317–420	
Southern and northern dynasties	*Southern dynasties:*		
	Song	420–479	
	Qi	479–502	
	Liang	502–557	
	Chen	557–589	
	Northern dynasties:		
	Northern Wei	386–534	
	Eastern Wei	534–550	
	Western Wei	535–557	
	Northern Qi	550–577	
	Northern Zhou	557–580	
Sui		581–618	
Tang		618–907	690–705 Wu Zetian Interregnum: Zhou
Five Dynasties	Late Liang	907–923	904–979 Ten
	Late Tang	923–936	Kingdoms in the
	Late Jin	936–947	south
	Late Han	947–950	
	Late Zhou	950–960	
Song	Northern Song	960–1127	Foreign dynasties:
	Southern Song	1127–1279	Liao (916–1125), Western Xia (1032–1227) and Jin (1115–1234) in the north
Yuan (Mongols)		1279–1368	
Ming		1368–1644	
Qing (Manchurians)		1644–1911	

Women fishing (propaganda poster, 1978)

deceased's actual biography, the images were basically selected to document Confucian-inspired liberality.

Hardship and Revolt

The social situation often looked different in reality. During the second century—the same period when the idea of Confucian liberality was spreading—the gap between rich and poor became particularly striking. While the wealth of the landowning upper class grew enormously, small farmers (who were actually taxed most heavily) lived at the lowest subsistence level. A failed harvest meant they had to rely on loans. The landowners, who formed an alliance of the prosperous with civil servants and merchants, were quite willing to provide loans, only to repossess the land quickly in the usually predictable cases when the farmers were unable to repay.

> While the wealthy [landowners] who make a surplus become richer and richer, the penniless [peasants], who have no durable resources, get poorer and poorer. . . . They lack food and clothing . . . , and each failed harvest forces them . . . to sell their wives and children.
>
> *Zhenglun* (around 150), chapter 1

These consolidation processes were repeated in a constant rhythm throughout the course of Chinese history, and led, not surprisingly, to recurrent unrest. According to official historiography in the second century, there was a peasant revolt every four years on average. The actual incidence was probably even higher. There was no lack of well-meaning advice on combating rural poverty, but the imperial court was often too weak—or unwilling—to institute lasting reforms.

> Wealthy families have huge estates. . . . The poor who work in the fields suffer from hunger, while the rich have an easy life, fill their bellies, indulge and enjoy themselves, and moan about taxes.
>
> *Jiayou ji* (1055), chapter 5

It was the communists who first succeeded in breaking the power of "the landlords and their bailiffs" on a more permanent basis. The initial attempts occurred just a few years after the party was founded, when the peasant associations gained control of rural areas in several provinces, although not without massive use of terror. Mao Zedong commended this (along with many an act of vandalism) in a 1927 report on the situation in his home province, Hunan (*Hunan nongmin yundong kaocha baogao*). Mao was pleased by the modest attitude of the revolutionary masses in relation to their own needs and praised them for

THE GREAT FAMINE DISASTERS OF THE
NINETEENTH AND TWENTIETH CENTURIES

1876–1879	11 million dead
1896–1897	5 million dead
1928–1930	10 million dead
1959–1961	30 million dead

Figures for all victims are rough estimates.

obtaining firewood for cooking by chopping up sacred figurines from monasteries.

The euphoria, however, did not last long; the "revolutionary avant-garde" was soon forced to yield to the pressure of the troops led by Chiang Kaishek and had to withdraw from the "liberated" areas. It took until the establishment of the People's Republic in 1949 to open up a new opportunity—this time for the whole country. Yet after only a decade of consolidation there was a huge setback. The Great Leap Forward, designed to accelerate industrial production, and the establishment of people's communes and the denunciation of specialist knowledge resulted in neglect of agriculture and rapidly led to serious shortages.

> Lavish drinking sprees were forbidden everywhere. In Shaoshan, Xiangtan district, the order was given that guests should only be served three dishes—chicken, fish, and pork. Consumption of bamboo shoots, seaweed, and glass noodles was also banned.
>
> *Hunan nongmin yundong kaocha baogao* (1927), p. 37

Unimpressed by the first bad news, Mao Zedong reacted irritably, "This just means there will be a bit less pork for a while" (*Lushan huiyi shilu*, p. 170). He simply was not prepared to face up to the results of political errors. The outcome was the worst famine in Chinese history, a disaster that claimed the lives of at least 30 million people, particularly children and the aged. In some regions elementary schools stayed closed for a long period: No pupils were left to teach. The trauma these events caused was intensified because the men in power ordained silence and there was no opportunity to give vent to the pain. Even worse, the "three bitter years" quickly gave way to the "ten lost years." To be sure, people's existence during the Cultural Revolution proclaimed in 1966 was threatened less by lack of nutrition than by extreme acts of violence, but the mass of the population lived in very harsh conditions, and the dreary cooking matched the intellectual subjugation.

The situation in many parts of the country—particularly in the east—has improved dramatically since the reforms of the 1980s, with

MAJOR EVENTS IN TWENTIETH-CENTURY CHINA

1900	Boxer Rebellion
1912	Proclamation of the Republic
1937–1945	Sino-Japanese War
1946–1949	Civil War
1949	Proclamation of the People's Republic
1953–1956	Agricultural collectivization
1958–1962	Great Leap Forward
1966–1976	Cultural Revolution
1978	Start of reform policy
1989	Suppression of democracy movement
1992	Resumption of reform policy

enormous growth rates for many agricultural products. This was accompanied, however, by a sharp turn away from basic foodstuffs and toward luxury goods. In other words, wine instead of beans. Indirectly as well, there was a discernible trend away from a primarily subsistence-based agrarian economy, because the concentration on higher potato and corn yields was less to satisfy people's need for carbohydrates than to meet the rising demand for pig feed caused by increased meat consumption. Moreover, conditions in the countryside were hardly idyllic. Poverty was far from eradicated, and in many places thuggish landlords were merely replaced by corrupt functionaries. In retrospect, this makes certain statements from the 1950s and 1960s about the living standards of future generations look more like utopia than serious prognosis.

It is widely known that some cadres enjoyed a fine lifestyle even in times of crisis. When, however, leading officials such as Tan Zhenlin, who was responsible for agriculture in the central committee of the Communist Party, was publicly quoted extolling gastronomic extravagance, this scandalous denial of reality could literally be described as "hard to stomach"—particularly if we remember that Tan Zhenlin was an old comrade-in-arms of Mao's and a prime mover in the Great Leap Forward.

Monkey's brains could scarcely be described as a favorite dish for most of the population. In fact, in relation to some dishes regarded as delicacies in the south, many people in other parts of China share the disgust felt by Europeans. There are important regional differences in culinary

> What does Communism mean? . . . First of all, good food. It's not enough to simply eat your fill. At each meal . . . there should be chicken, pork, fish or eggs, . . . and monkey's brains, swallows' nests and cloud-ear mushrooms should be served when required.
>
> Tan Zhenlin, cited in the Red Guards' newspaper, *Hongqi*, March 21, 1967

tastes, and the persistent allegation that the Chinese eat anything that has four legs and isn't a table generally relates to the way people in Beijing describe the Cantonese. By now, however, the Cantonese have got used to refuting that, and may even be heard to retort that everything that moves in the sky or in water is edible—except airplanes and submarines.

When foods seem strange, distaste may be partly offset by their supposedly healthful effect—particularly when it comes to treating loss of men's potency or women's beauty. In this respect, the north is definitely not prepared to yield advantage to the south in satisfying the fleshly desires: The main branch of the restaurant chain *Guolizhuang* (literally, "pep in the pot"), where the menu specializes in male genitals, from donkey's penis to sheep's testicles, is not in Canton but in Beijing.

> South of the Yangzi, the puffer fish is the greatest delicacy. . . . To demonstrate extravagance, does one really have to make use of a creature [whose poison is] capable of killing a person? One can feast on it, but one can just as well do without it.
>
> *Xianqing ouji* (1671), chapter 12

Finally, Chinese menus pose a special challenge. They are often of limited help when ordering the dishes, and may lead to all kinds of surprises. Even indigenous Chinese customers can be caught out: Given the powers of imagination, the names invented for dishes often say more about the literary ambitions of the host than about the ingredients and gastronomic aspirations of the cooking. There are also particular conventions, of course. If "dragon and phoenix" are on the menu, you can generally expect fish and chicken—or maybe snake and quail. . . .

> I'll never let anybody talk me into thinking that snake flesh tastes like chicken. I've lived in China for forty years and never eaten snake, nor have any of my relatives.
>
> *Lin Yutang* 1935: 404.

Remains and Recipes

China can look back on a tradition of more than 3,000 years of writing, during which the knowledge of each period was recorded on materials such as animal bones, bronze vessels, wood panels, stone pillars, silk, and paper. In the first place, people learned written communication not to set down recipes but to codify religious practice, and above all to record consultation of oracles. Where matters connected with foodstuffs were documented before the founding of the empire in 221 B.C., this usually concerned agriculture and proper execution of rituals rather than culinary delights. Still, the *Zhaohun*, an early source from the turn of the century 4–3 B.C., tells us that people back then feasted on ox cutlets, turtle ragout, honey cake, and beer chilled with ice; and the chapter "*Daya*" in *Shijing*, a much earlier work, offers readers a first glimpse into the rules of etiquette.

Correct behavior was also the main topic of two classic compendia of rules, *Zhouli* and *Liji*, compiled in the first and second centuries A.D. Both works are based on earlier sources, but they tend to glorify and do not necessarily convey the real picture of the Zhou dynasty. However, the regulations they contain are far from historically irrelevant; they attest indirectly to the fact that conventions 2,000 years ago were obligatory to only a limited extent, and this led to the need to compensate for the lack of good manners by building up "tradition" creatively.

The *Liji, The Book of Rites,* discussed which tasks had to be carried out month by month at court and throughout the kingdom, and the right kind of diet for the changing seasons of the year. On the basis of this timescale, manuals offering concrete help to farmers were compiled from early on. It began in the mid–second century A.D. with the *Simin yueling*, which described the most important activities on a farm, including conserving food and making alcoholic beverages. Cooking recipes, however, were first included in the *Qimin yaoshu*, written around 400 years later, which contained lengthy passages explaining how to prepare various dishes, from pickled vegetables and millet mush to cured meat. This was interspersed with practical tips on how to stop food from sticking to the pot, or how to prevent pest infestation.

The custom of sticking to exact measurements for the ingredients was probably not established until the Song period. The *Wushi zhongkuilu* is widely regarded as the oldest existing collection of recipes that enabled readers to reproduce the dishes described. This slim volume is attributed to a "Mrs. Wu," who is thought to have lived in the eastern coastal region in the thirteenth century. It is not always easy, however, to distinguish

> Eating of young soft-shelled turtles should [basically] be avoided. [In addition, one should] remove: the intestines of the wolf, the kidneys of the dog, the straight spine of the wildcat, the rump of the hare, the head of the fox, the brains of the sucking-pig. . . .
>
> *"Neize"* chapter in the *Liji* (second century B.C.)

clearly between recipe books and works intended as manuals for healthy nutrition rather than as guides to making tasty dishes. Ultimately, dietetics was at the heart of Chinese medicine, with its strong emphasis on prevention, and this is reflected linguistically in Chinese by the

SELECTED AGRICULTURAL MANUALS WITH INFORMATION ON FOOD AND DRINK

Title	Author/compiler	Date
Simin yueling	Cui Shi	around 160
Qimin yaoshu	Jia Sixie	around 540
Gengzhitu	Lou Shou	1145
Nongshu	Chen Fu	1149
Nongsang jiayao	Meng Qi (?)	1273
Nongshu	Wang Chen	1313
Nongsang yishi cuoyao	Lu Mingshan	around 1314
Nongzheng quanshu	Xu Guangqi	1628
Shoushi tongkao	E'ertai	1742

double meaning of the term *recipe*, which is also used for a medicinal prescription.

A wealth of Chinese treatises exists on the consumption of tea and alcohol. Cultivating a good lifestyle is obviously the main issue, but along with this a whole series of studies through the ages is concerned with choosing ingredients carefully, setting the table correctly, and following the right procedure for drinking. Classic examples dealing with tea include the *Chajing* (760), the *Daguan chalun* (1107), and the *Chaju tuzan* (1269). Works devoted to alcoholic beverages include the *Jiujing* (1090), the *Beishan Jiujing* (1117), and the *Shangzheng* (1606). The tone of these writings may sometimes be solemn and ponderous, but often we find a refreshing touch of irony as well, and some daring satires even entertain readers with bawdy humor.

The information in compendia written by and for specialists sometimes reveals less than descriptions in literary works such as novels, short stories, travelogues, or "notebooks" (a literary genre combining different kinds of prose variations without a fixed form). For instance, some descriptions of cities from the Song period contain lengthy passages about the variety of foods on sale at markets and the truly enormous number of dishes served in the taverns. Particularly instructive, despite the occasional tendency to subjective exaggeration, are poems dealing with innumerable aspects of daily life—although the passion for tea and alcoholic beverages is evident far more often than appreciation of good food.

Transmission of the official heritage was the responsibility of historiographers, a group of experts in the scribal tradition who recorded oracle consultation at the end of the second millennium B.C. A slight tendency to soothsaying in the imperial age is also discernible; after all, chroniclers were not really obliged to document the course of events accurately. Instead, they were supposed to formulate paradigms to provide guidance for future generations, if necessary by excluding or distorting reality. To some extent this reservation also applies to many of the encyclopedias compiled for the court. Although they illuminated the formal mentality of an epoch, they did not explain how this was embedded in political and social life. They were handbooks, and generally tailored to preparing for the civil service examinations that governed admission into public service.

Beyond the official version of history, a variety of texts—including local chronicles, collections of statutes, legal codices, and farmers' almanacs—presented plain information rather than well-worded ethical advice. Dealing with these sources is hampered by the fact that they have almost all been handed down only in versions that are the end results of a long historical chain. In fact, no archives have survived continuously back to the unification of the empire. The exception to this is texts that were carved in stone to give them permanence.

> Two deadbeats were talking about their life's goal. One said to the other, "All I need is nosh and sleep. Even if I managed to make good now, I'd still spend my time either noshing or snoozing." The other replied, "Then we're totally different: I'd just stick to eating, which would leave no time for sleeping."
>
> *Dongbo zhilin* (1101), chapter 1

Apart from epigraphic records, for some time now a considerable number of increasingly important writings have been found among funerary objects from the early imperial period. They enable comparisons with the previously known versions and include a whole series of treatises on dietetics. Cookbooks were also deposited in the graves. For example, the tomb of Wu Yang, who was buried in 162 B.C. in today's Yuanling (Hunan province), contained notes for more than 150 recipes, mainly instructions for preparing meat, written on around 300 bamboo strips.

In addition, various kinds of records giving insight into the life of the local population have been preserved in the northwestern border garrisons and in Buddhist monasteries. Even more revealing are the wall paintings in the cave complexes mainly constructed in the Tang period (618–907) in the border areas of Gobi and Taklamakan. Alongside religious themes, the paintings depict the everyday life of monks and lay people. In some places the monasteries had regular treasure chambers.

SELECTED COOKBOOKS WITH LARGE RECIPE SECTIONS

Title	Author/compiler	Date
Wushi zhongkuilu	Wushi ("Mrs. Wu")	1st half of 13th century
Benxinzhai shushipu	Chen Dasou	around 1250
Shilin guangji	Chen Yuanjing	around 1280
Shanjia qinggong	Lin Hong	2nd half of 13th century
Yinshan zhengyao	Hu Sihui	1330
Jujia biyong shilei quanji	(?)	1st half of 14th century
Yi Ya yiyi	Han Yi	1st half of 14th century
Yunlintang yinshi zhidu ji	Ni Zan	1360
Yinzhuan fushi jian	Gao Lian	1591
Xianqing ouji	Li Yu	1671
Shixian hongmi	Zhu Yizun	1680
Yang xiaolu	Gu Zhong	1698
Tiaoding ji	Tong Yuejian (?)	around 1765 with later additions
Suiyuan shidan	Yuan Mei	1790

For example, an "underground palace" containing numerous precious objects, most of which were donated by the royal family, was discovered in the foundations of a pagoda belonging to the Famen Temple (Shaanxi province). The find included tableware and various requisites for preparing tea. Hoard finds occur relatively seldom in China. Either people were reluctant to entrust the family fortune to a hiding place in times of crisis or there was a relatively high rate of finds, whether the valuables were retrieved by the owners or by thieves. There are, however, exceptions such as the Hejiacun complex (Shaanxi province), which contained countless gold and silver objects. The plates, bowls, flat dishes, and jugs give a glimpse of the pleasures of dining in style in the eighth century.

Most of the clues for reconstructing living conditions during the premodern era are found in tombs, which were frequently decorated with a facing of relief tiles or engraved flagstones, or covered with large painted areas. Aside from mythological subjects, we can often identify everyday settings, including some kitchen scenes. Effigies, mostly of clay, were also placed in the tombs, and included figurines of people and animals, and miniatures of storage buildings, privies, animal pens, wells, mills, and stoves. Vessels for eating and drinking were often part of the offerings, and the choice of materials was ultimately supposed to signify the deceased person's social status.

Foodstuffs were often discovered among the archeological remains, and sometimes a complete pantry was found in the grave. One really important legacy to mention here was discovered in Tomb 1 of the Ma-wangdui Tombs (Hunan province). Dating back to around 167 B.C., aside from huge quantities of food, it contained records that allow us to ascertain the names given at the time to the dishes deposited there. There is actually much earlier evidence of inventory lists with similar information, such as that from a burial in Baoshan (Hubei province) dating back to the fourth century B.C. that enables us to replicate a "menu" that included roast pork, fish stew, and honey plums. In this case, however, it is impossible to establish any direct link with zoological or botanical remains.

Finally, ancient picture scrolls and album sheets constitute an important source of information, although most have only survived as later copies. Even if their authenticity is doubtful, we shouldn't simply dismiss them as evidence, because originals were handled rather informally in China, and any artist of note was expected to be able to copy sensitively. Book printing, which greatly increased the spread of knowledge from the Song period onward, led not only to standardization of texts but also to relatively unified design of illustrations. Anyhow, the dividing lines between the different media were, and still are, not always sharply defined. The claim that Wang Wei (699–759) created "poems that give the feeling of pictures, and pictures that evoke associations with poems" (*Mojie shi Lantian yanyu tu*) applies not just to that particular artist, who was famous as a universal genius, but also to many members of the educated elites of every period.

Chapter Two

A Taste of Harmony

Staple Food: Cereals and Tubers

In China, people eat rice. This is not just a well-worn platitude—it happens to be true. China is, after all, the world's biggest rice producer. Yet even with increasing use of hybrid varieties that boost the harvest by 15 to 20 percent, the country cannot guarantee to supply enough rice for its 1.35 billion inhabitants. For some time now the government has been forced to supplement homegrown stocks with imports. Moreover, the rice hybrids put farmers in a risky situation of dependency: Since the subsequent generations of plants do not breed true, seed stock has to be reproduced from scratch every time.

The hybrid varieties can be divided into two groups: long narrow grains, which swell substantially, and oval to round grains, which absorb much less water in cooking. Both groups include varieties that develop a sticky consistency during cooking because of their relatively large dextrin and amylopectin contents. For obvious reasons, this is called "sticky," or glutinous, rice. The Chinese language has far more clearly differentiated and complex terms for rice. Aside from innumerable regional appellations and specific botanical features, there are two major factors: the kind of cultivation area (dry land or irrigated terraces) and the timescale for sowing and reaping (early or late).

> (1) Only good quality, carefully husked rice . . . should be used. (2) This should be washed thoroughly . . . until completely clear water drips from the basket [used for washing]. (3) Start cooking at a high temperature, then reduce to low heat. (4) To achieve the right consistency, do not add too much or too little water.
>
> *Suiyuan shidan* (1790), chapter 13

Winnowing (wall painting, tenth century)

Since the Han period, the milling process in China has consisted not only of "shelling" or peeling the rice after threshing (by removing the hull) but also of "polishing," which means taking off the bran layer so that the grain cooks faster and is more easily digestible. The disadvantage of polishing is that valuable nutrients are lost in the process, especially vitamin B1, which helps prevent beriberi, a vitamin deficiency disease.

In the pre-Christian millennia, rice was cultivated mainly, but not exclusively, in the south of the country, whereas two other cereals, proso millet and foxtail millet, predominated in the north. The grains from both types of millet have high protein content and are rich in vitamins and minerals, including silicon, magnesium, potassium, and iron. The hulls are usually removed because the seed coat tastes bitter and contains less well-tolerated substances such as phytic acid and oxalic acid.

Millet farming barely features in the economy of present-day China. Moreover, agricultural statistics for the twenty-first century hardly mention the production of a number of other cereals and pseudo-cereals that achieved transregional importance in the course of history. These include sorghum, barley, oats, buckwheat, Job's tears, and white goosefoot. Hempseed, which was categorized as a cereal crop in traditional

Chinese plant classification, is another crop that has lost its place in human nutrition.

The growth rate for farming of wheat has risen significantly in the past several decades, and despite the recent stagnation, China remains by far the world's largest wheat producer. Yet the enormous demand still means that the country often has to rely on imports. Cultivation of wheat, like rice, probably dates back to prehistoric times, but reliable evidence for this exists only since the Han period, when the grain was mostly processed into flour and made into noodle dough.

Corn, or maize, originated in America and reached the Middle Kingdom as early as the sixteenth century along with European expansion. It took considerable time until it became an important economic factor in China, at first in the southwest of the country and later almost everywhere. China is presently the world's second largest corn producer. It is difficult to determine the importance of corn for the national food supply because the share of corn exported is higher than that for any other cereal crop. Note that only a relatively small part of the corn harvest goes directly to feed humans. Huge quantities are used for animal food, and the growing demand for meat is probably the major reason that croplands for corn have increased, unlike those for rice and wheat. In any case, future utilization of corn will focus increasingly on its potential for producing bioenergy.

Aside from cereals, a variety of tuberous plants are cultivated in China for their high starch content. Taro and yams were already grown in prehistoric times, whereas cultivation of the sweet potato and potato only began in the sixteenth century. Taro, in particular, was an important part of the diet for a long period, not only for survival in hard times but also as a specialty at the imperial court. However, production has

Rice (book illustration, 1609)

Wheat is bestowed on us:
as fine as jade dust
and sprinklings of powdery snow—
heavenly moisture turned to crystal.

Benxinzhai shushipu (around 1250), chapter 1

GRAIN YIELDS (IN MILLIONS OF METRIC TONS) FROM 1980 TO 2005

	Rice	Wheat	Corn	Other
1980	134	55	63	62
1985	169	86	64	61
1990	189	98	97	62
1995	185	102	112	17
2000	188	100	106	12
2005	181	97	139	10

fallen greatly since the introduction of plants from the New World. This trend has increased in recent years, and today more potatoes are grown in China than all the other tuberous plants together. Though it may not be obvious from Chinese eating habits, the country is the world's largest producer of potatoes and sweet potatoes. Incidentally, taro and yams should be cooked slowly to wash out the toxins contained in the tubers. Ideally, the cooking water should be changed several times.

Fruit and Vegetables: Fresh Is Best

Pulses are an important part of the diet, especially because the ripe seeds are rich in protein and relatively high yields can be achieved on fairly small crop areas. Traditionally, the most popular leguminous plants in

Arable farming (clay tile painting, third century)

China are the azuki bean, the rice bean, the mung bean, and the fava bean. Some young varieties, such as peas, are eaten whole with the pod. Bean sprouts (particularly from the mung bean) are very popular for their crisp, fresh texture and high nutritional value.

The tender sprouts of the soybean are a staple of the Chinese diet. In fact, soybeans have a special status among the legumes: They can be processed into a wide variety of products, including milk and curd. This is done by soaking the beans in water until they swell, then pureeing and sieving them to yield a protein-rich liquid. Soy milk is drinkable and can be congealed using a coagulant such as gypsum. The water is squeezed out, leaving a mass with a more or less solid form, depending on the degree of pressure. The Chinese word for the bean curd produced by this type of method is *doufu*, but it is generally known in the West by the Japanese name, tofu. The variation comes from different pronunciations of the same characters. Their literal meaning is "rotten beans"—which does not really reflect their enormous importance in a country where many people rely on a vegetarian diet.

BEAN CURD WITH MINCED PORK (SICHUAN)

Ingredients

8 oz (250 g) minced pork
3 tbsp soy sauce
2 tbsp rice wine
5 tbsp peanut oil, 1 tbsp sesame oil
1 cup chopped scallions
1 tbsp chopped ginger root
1 tbsp chopped fresh chilies
2 tbsp bean sauce
18 oz (500 g) diced bean curd (*doufu*)
4 fl oz (125 ml) chicken stock
2 tbsp cornstarch dissolved in 4 tbsp cold water
2 tsp roasted Sichuan peppercorns

Preparation method

1. Combine the ground pork, soy sauce, and rice wine.
2. Heat the mixture of peanut and sesame oil.
3. Stir-fry the pork mixture quickly in the oil.
4. Add the scallions, ginger, chilies, bean sauce, bean curd, and chicken stock.
5. Thicken with the cornstarch solution, stirring constantly.
6. Season with Sichuan peppercorns.

Soybeans are also used to make a variety of seasoning pastes and condiments. Meanwhile, soybeans, like rapeseed, are being increasingly used as the basis for producing biofuels. This is the main reason that China has been importing huge quantities for some time now. The market share of soybeans in the production of edible oil has tended to fall in recent years, whereas sales of fats from peanuts, sunflowers, and other plants originally indigenous only to the American continent have risen.

Although pumpkin seed oil does not play a significant role in Chinese cooking, large quantities of the seeds of various pumpkin types have been exported in recent years, not least to Austria, where they are used to make so-called original Styrian pumpkin seed oil. The plants are mostly grown for their tasty seeds. The winter melon is often hollowed out and used as a dish to hold food; the bottle gourd is used as a calabash. Another member of the gourd family, the cucumber, is very popular as well, not only as an ingredient in many dishes but also artistically carved as decoration. The historical cultivation of the eggplant in China can be traced very far back, but it was not until European expansion that other members of the nightshade, or potato, family, arrived in the country, including the pepper, the chili, and the tomato, which the Chinese call "barbarian eggplant."

See Appendix, Table 1.

Bamboo shoots have been an integral part of Chinese cooking for more than 2,000 years. The shoots of the various bamboo genera are dug out in spring or winter and taste best shortly after harvesting, but to neutralize the toxins they contain, they should be cooked before being eaten. However, good-quality preserved varieties exist that can be steamed, fried, pickled, or prepared in other ways to maximize their high nutritional value.

The rhizomes of the Indian lotus are toxin-free. The root is usually cut into slices and then boiled, steamed, or deep-fried. It can also be eaten raw, pickled, dried, or made into flour. The lotus, a water plant, was adopted as a symbol by Buddhists and Daoists. In addition to the rhizome, the shoots, leaves, and flower buds are edible; so are the nuts, but only after removing the pericarp and the bitter embryo. Another common cultivated water plant is the water chestnut, a marsh plant. The tubers are peeled to reveal a firm white flesh known for its crispy consistency and sweetish flavor. Alternatively, the starch it contains can be used to make a kind of flour.

The other main root vegetables are radishes and carrots. They can both be prepared in a variety of ways: fried, boiled,
braised, or pickled, for instance. They are
also ideal for decoration, and it is a nice
surprise to find your plate garnished with
cranes carved from vegetables. The carrot reached China relatively late, which is

> When talking about the quality of veg-
> etables, people [generally] resort to
> terms like "pure," "flawless," "aromatic,"
> or "crunchy." This misses the point that
> their advantage over any kind of meat
> can be summed up in just one word:
> freshness.
>
> *Xianqing ouji* (1671), chapter 12

why it is still known there as "barbarian radish." This term actually rep-
resents a successful integration story, because the radish was originally
an exotic plant and had only been indigenous to the country for a few
centuries by the time the carrot arrived.

Leeks and other onion family plants grow almost everywhere in
China, but a number of dietary works categorize them as "pungent-
smelling," and some Buddhist schools prohibit their consumption. Numerous archaeological finds and written sources confirm that most of
the *Allium* species were farmed at least from the Han period, if not earlier. Onions, shallots, and chives, however, were introduced much later.

The most predominant leaf vegetables are various kinds of cabbage
plants, including bok choy and white cabbage. They can be used in different ways; although they are best eaten soon after harvesting, there
are various preservation methods, especially pickling in brine or vinegar.
Two other vegetables worth mentioning are celery and amaranth. Spinach, which is the basis of some food colorings, only reached China by
the Silk Road under the Tang dynasty.

See Appendix, Table 2.

Various species of kelp and seaweed are among the plants that enrich
the diet with valuable vitamins and minerals (such as calcium and iron).
The thalli, or bodies of the plants, are eaten; they are generally dried and
used as a soup vegetable. Cultivating seaweed has been a major priority in China for the past several decades. Production increased over six
times from 1980 to 2005, and the potential is far from exhausted.

Mushrooms are traditional items in the food cupboard, especially in
the south of the country. The jelly ear, a secondary parasite that grows on
trees, is generally sold in dried form and should be thoroughly washed
before soaking in warm water. It is better known in the West as "cloud
ear mushroom" and "Chinese morel." Portions should be measured on
the small side, because they swell to at least double the original size. The

same applies to the snow fungus, or "silver ear," which grows on rotten trees and is increasingly cultivated artificially on wood-based substrate. The mushroom commonly known in Europe by its Japanese name, shiitake, is usually sold in dried form, but Chinese cooks prefer it fresh. The oyster mushroom and button mushroom have only been grown in large quantities in recent decades, both for rising domestic consumption and for export.

The enormous rise in fruit production is also largely due to the export trade. Domestic demand too is much greater than it was several decades ago. Of course, this is partly a result of improved living standards for a growing section of the population. There is an obvious parallel with the Song dynasty, when members of the affluent upper stratum demonstrated their wealth by eating increased quantities of fresh fruit. *See Appendix, Table 3.*

Certain fruits merit special mention because they have an archetypal function in Chinese cooking, although they are hardly known in the West. One example is the jujube, an elongated, red-colored stone fruit grown particularly in the north of the country. Its cultivation in ancient times

is exceptionally well documented. The lychee, which has long been grown mainly in the south, is easily recognizable by its rough skin, whose color ranges from red to brown, depending on ripeness. The longan is smaller, much smoother, and lighter in color. The canned varieties are often dominated by a syrupy taste, and it is difficult to distinguish between the two fruits in cans because both have translucent white flesh. The lychee is generally considered superior. The loquat, which is usually yellow, comes from the central region between Huanghe and Yangzi. A pip fruit distantly related to the apple, it is also known as the Japanese medlar.

Although pineapple and papaya have been cultivated in China for only a few centuries, it seems almost impossible to imagine today's market stalls without them. Berry fruits still play only a minor

Jujube (book illustration, 1609)

GLAZED APPLES (BEIJING, SHANDONG)

Ingredients

3 firm, tart apples, peeled, cored and each cut into 8 wedges
Batter: ⅔ cup (100 g) flour, 1 beaten egg, and ½ cup (⅛ L) water
¾ cup (150 g) sugar
2 tbsp sesame seeds

Preparation method

1. Toss the apple wedges in the batter, fry in batches and keep warm.
2. Pour off the oil, leaving only a thin film, and caramelize the sugar in it.
3. Add the apple wedges, sprinkle with the sesame seeds and mix well.
4. Leave on a plate to cool, and serve while still warm.

Note: This dessert can be made with fruits other than apples. You can substitute hot honey for the melted sugar.

role in China, except for mulberries (which are grown mainly for the leaves needed for breeding silkworms), and grapes. Much of the grape harvest today is used for alcohol production. Otherwise, the Chinese prefer drinking their fruit juice freshly squeezed and unfermented. Stewed fruit is also common, as are preserves made with honey or sugar, fruit preserved in syrup, and dried fruit products.

See Appendix, Table 4.

Fruits are used as standard motifs in the visual arts and poetry in China. In fact, many fruits have symbolic meanings that often hark back to a long tradition and still have an impact on present-day social conventions. It is important to bear this in mind, particularly when choosing fresh fruits to give as gifts, which is a common custom. Many fruits are associated with specific wishes or desires, such as luck (loquats, oranges), peace (apples), fertility (pomegranate, plum, melon), longevity (peach, pear), and female beauty and sexuality (apricot, cherry), and the receivers may interpret the gift as a hidden message.

From time to time, new fruits become symbols. One example is a story dating back to 1968, when Mao Zedong received seven mangos as a gift from the visiting Pakistani foreign minister. Mao ordered the mangos to be distributed to the propaganda troops who were stepping up their campaign in Beijing against the disgraced Red Guards. For a short time, the implied endorsement led to mangos achieving a kind of cult

Melon vendor in Beijing (1955)

status that became totally irrational, but evaporated just as quickly after the end of the Cultural Revolution. In that brief period, however, the mango had occupied a very unique position, and in the capital, where the mood was very severe, a person could receive draconian penalties merely for the cheeky remark that a lot of fuss was going on about a sort of fruit that was actually quite common in the south of the country.

Status and Distaste: Animal Products

Meat consumption is one of the clearest indicators of status. While chicken and duck dominated the seven main courses of an imperial court menu in the year 1754, large sections of the population lived on a vegetarian diet nearly the whole year round. Some did this out of religious conviction, but most did it for economic reasons. Leaving aside the heated debates about the pros and cons of vegetarianism, we should remember that in eighteenth-century China a chicken cost nearly as much as 7 kilograms of rice. Even in the 1920s and 1930s, average per capita meat consumption was only around 35 grams per day.

Cock and Pig (clay figurines, second century)

In China, the domestic pig has held pride of place among animals kept for meat production since the Neolithic age, and in some periods it accounted for nearly 90 percent of meat consumption. Large numbers of clay miniatures found in graves from the Han period illustrate how swine, which were generally fed with kitchen waste, were kept in sties. The models often show privies inside the fenced pigsty enclosure, which gives an added twist to the notion of recycling (but seems dubious in hygienic terms). The fact that pork is usually washed before cooking can hardly allay worries on that score.

Pig's innards are a great delicacy. The intestines are served with a variety of fillings and as a cold starter. Along with the liver, kidneys, heart, and lung, they are believed to be very effective in healing various ailments; to some extent this also applies to ham, which is made by brining the leg of pork in salt and then smoking it. Finally, in some regions lard is used for stir-frying, or added to cooked foods.

> Meat eaters are simple-minded . . . , because they completely lack the capacity for reflection, whereas any living creature that feeds on plants is resourceful and clever. . . . By contrast, the tiger, which only eats meat, is the most stupid animal in existence. . . . That is what many books say.
>
> *Xianqing ouji* (1671), chapter 12

> On the assumption that the tastiest pigs were kept in Qianyang [now Shaanxi province], I sent a man there to get one. But [after buying a particularly fine pig] my servant got drunk [and fell asleep], and the pig ran away, so he replaced it with another [inferior] one. I didn't notice anything myself, and my dinner guests exclaimed in astonishment at the unique quality [of the meat]. When the truth came out, however, it was very embarrassing.
>
> Ba Wangshi huayanjing jie (1075)

Cow (book illustration, 1609)

Dishes involving the meat of cattle or wild water buffalo play a minor role in traditional cooking, although Chinese restaurant menus in the West usually give a different impression. Some population groups avoid this type of meat altogether on principle. The remarkable rise in cattle production in recent decades is mostly due to improved living standards. One way for members of the new upper class to celebrate their prosperity is to have steak for dinner more often.

Sheep and goats are farmed on a large scale, particularly in northwestern China. This is partly due to favorable geographical and climatic conditions for the pastoral economy, but also because the region has a large Muslim population with a religious prohibition on eating pork. In addition, horses, donkeys, camels, and yaks are bred, especially in the plateaus and steppes on the country's periphery, but this has only a local significance for the food supply.

To some extent this also applies to dairy products, which have traditionally played a minor role in the south, due not least to the lactose intolerance that affects well over 90 percent of the population, an even higher proportion than in the north. Despite this, the growing trend toward a Western-type lifestyle resulted in production of cow's milk increasing nearly twentyfold in the period from 1980 to 2005.

Take thirty pounds of dog meat and six pint measures each of wheat and clear alcohol. Bring these ingredients to the boil three times, then pour off the [remaining] liquid and [start again] by adding three pint measures each of wheat and clear alcohol. Boil everything again until the dog meat separates from the bones. Finally, mix in thirty beaten eggs, pour the mixture into a sack and steam it till the egg has a firm consistency. Press out [the remaining liquid] with a stone, and leave overnight before serving.

Qimin yaoshu (around 540), chapter 9

In China, unlike in some other parts of the world, it was not just the poor who ate the flesh of the dog in hard times, or as regular food. According to tradition, dog meat was a standard feature on the imperial court menu for special occasions, and there are written sources for a whole

BEEF WITH SESAME SEEDS (HEBEI)

Ingredients

10 oz (300 g) lean beef
1 oz (25 g) shiitake mushrooms (soak for 30 minutes in warm water, then remove
   the stalks and cut into thin strips)
3 tbsp soy sauce
1 tbsp rice wine
1 tsp ground chili pepper
1 tsp finely chopped ginger
1 tsp finely chopped garlic
5 tbsp toasted sesame seeds
2 tbsp peanut oil
1 tbsp sesame oil
3 finely chopped scallions, white parts only

Preparation method

1. Combine the meat, mushrooms, soy sauce, rice wine, ground hot pepper,
   ginger, garlic and sesame seeds and leave to stand for at least an hour.
2. Fry well in a mixture of the two oils.
3. Garnish with the scallions before serving.

series of different dishes, including "Dog soup with sticky rice," "Dog ragout," "Stew with dog meat and sow thistle," "Dog meat with hemp seeds or millet," and "Dog liver roasted in its own fat." This tradition still holds today. Despite a string of prohibitions at intervals from the very distant past onward, many people in twenty-first-century China still enjoy a dish of "fragrant meat" (the euphemism for dog).

Whereas dogs have been specially bred for eating and kept in pens, at least since the Han period, this seems never to have been the case for domestic cats. Today, market vendors, restaurants, and private consumers buy the animals from catchers who grab them on the street and sometimes in doorways, in gardens, or on balconies. These "mass cat kidnappings" have recently aroused growing protests in the big cities. Meanwhile, the lobby for rabbits has been less vocal.

Dog (clay figurine, second century)

Many rabbits vegetate in cage systems under very cramped conditions. While they are mainly bred for their skins, the production of rabbit meat is equally lucrative, and a good share of this meat lands in the freezer cabinets of supermarkets abroad.

The Chinese are not averse to game, but continual overhunting means that deer (including small species) and wild boar are served up much more rarely today than in ancient times. In some regions the meat of various species of monkey, particularly the macaques, is still regarded as a delicacy. This also applies to many rodents, although the Chinese bamboo rat has lost the culinary status it enjoyed back in the days when it was a specialty at the imperial court. Many members of the rodent family have a bad reputation as disease carriers, among them the civet, which is thought to be responsible for spreading severe acute respiratory syndrome (SARS).

There is also a very large selection of winged game; in fact, there are few birds that the Chinese do not eat, although domestic species generally predominate in the consumption of animal protein. The main example is the domestic fowl, which accounts for a major share of meat production. Duck is primarily associated with festive occasions, and there are elaborate recipes for its preparation throughout the country; the most famous, of course, is Peking duck. Aside from this, goose, pheasant, and quail have been important in the diet of the upper classes for at least 2,000 years. The Chinese eat fowl eggs, especially chicken's and duck's, but consumption is altogether much lower than in the West. There are a variety of methods for preserving the eggs.

See Appendix, Tables 5 and 6.

The fishing tradition in China dates back to the Neolithic period, as is demonstrated by plentiful finds of fish bones, fishing hooks, sinkers, and harpoons. There are also numerous surviving clay miniatures of ponds from the period of the unification of the kingdom in the third century B.C. They are apparently modeled on ponds made for breeding. Aside from fishing in rivers and lakes, irrigated paddy fields were also often used for aquaculture. As pollution takes its toll, fish hauls in some parts of the country have fallen far below the levels of thirty years ago.

> The main fish [bred in ponds] are gold-fish, grass carp, carp, black carp, and bleak. In some places . . . pavilions are built on the shores to give a view over the water.
>
> *Jiatai Kuaiji zhi* (1201), chapter 17

In southern China, tame cormorants are bred for a traditional form of fishing: A soft ring is fitted around their long necks to prevent them from swallowing their prey. The birds spew out their haul on their owner's boat or raft, and are rewarded with an occasional snack. However, the only purpose of this type of food-gathering nowadays is to attract tourists. Reports also exist of trained otters being used to flush out fish and drive them into nets.

Whereas the inhabitants of the coastal strip north of the Yangzi delta regarded it as the frontier to the inhospitable realm of the ocean for many centuries, the people who settled in the southeast of the country had a much easier relationship with the sea. This was particularly true of the local fishermen, who have cast their nets for centuries, mainly to catch varieties of herring, and preserve their wares by curing or drying, as in Europe. In tandem with the rising demand for fresh produce, fishing yields in recent years have also increased significantly, with corresponding effects on nature and consumers; the positive statistics are mostly due to a very sharp increase in aquaculture.

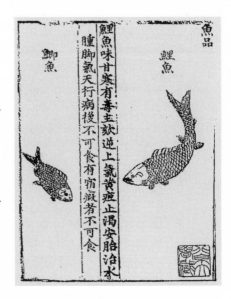

Carp (book illustration, 1330)

See Appendix, Table 7.

The increase in crustaceans, mussels, and snails is even more significant. This is due both to the lucrative outlook for exports and to rising living standards. The main crustaceans include prawns and spiny lobsters. Chinese mitten crabs and Asian paddle crabs are also important in economic terms.

SEAFOOD PRODUCE (IN THOUSANDS OF METRIC TONS) FROM 1980 TO 2005

	Fishing	Aquaculture	Fish	Crustaceans	Mollusks	Seaweeds
1980	86.4%	13.6%	2,341	421	234	262
1985	83.0%	17.0%	2,745	706	473	273
1990	77.3%	22.7%	4,231	1,070	1,473	275
1995	71.4%	28.6%	7,581	1,848	3,923	749
2000	58.2%	41.8%	10,330	2,971	10,387	1222
2005	51.2%	48.8%	10,520	3,238	11,604	1542

Fish breed rapidly, and it's almost impossible to exterminate them. . . . If humans didn't reduce the stock . . . , the numbers [of fish] would grow to incredible dimensions. [In the end] they could even narrow and block the rivers, and boats would no longer be able to get through. . . . This makes it easier [to justify] eating fish and crustaceans than other animals.

Xianqing ouji (1671), chapter 12

The trade in scallops used to be seasonal, and it is only fairly recently that various types of oysters reached the markets beyond the coastal areas. In the past the flesh of these sea products was seldom eaten raw. It was usually dried for preservation and transportability. Numerous other sea creatures were processed into seasoning sauces. The innards of the ear shell, a sea snail that cookbooks usually call "abalone," are too valuable for this; they are thought to be particularly good for health. The same applies to various long spiny echinoderms generally known in the West as "sea cucumbers." Along with shark fins and swallow's nests, they are some of the most expensive ingredients in Chinese cooking.

Traditional Chinese classification of fishes includes turtles and snakes, regardless of whether the animals live mainly on land or in water. The

SQUID WITH BEAN SAUCE (ZHEJIANG)

Ingredients

1½ lb (600 g) squid with head and tentacles removed (this will reduce the weight by around one-third), cleaned and washed thoroughly
2 chopped scallions, white parts only
5 chopped garlic cloves
1 tsp chopped ginger
1 medium hot chili, chopped
1 tbsp black bean sauce
1 tbsp cornstarch dissolved in 4 tbsp cold water and 1 tbsp oyster sauce
2 tbsp rice wine

Preparation method

1. Slice the squid open lengthways, score a diamond pattern on the inside and cut into pieces.
2. Blanch the squid pieces quickly in boiling water until they curl; then rinse with cold water.
3. Sauté the squid pieces briskly in oil, remove, and keep warm.
4. Stir-fry the scallions, garlic, ginger, and chili.
5. Mix in the bean sauce, then the squid pieces.
6. Add the starch solution and bring to the boil.
7. Add rice wine to taste, and serve immediately.

gelatinous mass from the underside of the turtle shell is considered a particular delicacy. Eating various kinds of turtle is said to promote longevity. As regards snakes, the borderline between culinary enjoyment, nutritional science, and imagination is rather hazy. The most spectacular delicacy is undoubtedly the king cobra, which can be up to 5 meters long. Other very popular edible snake varieties include spectacled cobras, Asian rat snakes, kraits, and sea snakes that inhabit coastal waters.

The Spices: Discretion and Delicacy

Fishermen (1955)

Five basic flavors have been distinguished in China since ancient times: sour, bitter, sweet, pungent, and salty. This classification is based on the five phases from which countless other five-element systems are derived, including an associated number of smells, organs, and emotions. In fact, the variety of aromas was obviously much greater, and the approach to spices was correspondingly subtle.

Salt was mainly extracted from the sea. In late imperial China, salt works in the coastal areas produced more than 80 percent of the salt. Parallel to this, the Chinese utilized natural crystallization of salt lakes in the interior, and constructed some artificial evaporation basins close to the shores. Finally, in southwestern China natural salt deposits were mined with bores that could reach down to a depth of more than 1,000 meters. By contrast, yields of ground salt and rock salt were relatively low. Another indicator of this mineral's importance is that salt tax sometimes accounted for nearly 80 percent of total tax revenues.

In Chinese cuisine, at least where traditional dishes are concerned, it is unusual for the guest to add salt. In fact, there is

> Salt is supposed to bring out the best in every other aroma without being perceptible itself. . . . If you use too much, it makes everything taste the same. Then nothing can save the dish, [however perfect] the cutting technique, the choice of ingredients, and the cooking temperature.
>
> *Meishijia* (1983), p. 35

Sugar cane (book illustration, 1742)

generally no possibility of that. The only condiment likely to be added after cooking is soy sauce, which contains a high level of sodium chloride. Incidentally, it is clear that as far back as we can trace, salt was used not just for seasoning, but also for preserving.

Pepper is processed in various ways; the main type used in Chinese cooking is the black pepper that was originally introduced from the neighboring southern countries, and is mostly farmed in the southwestern provinces today. Peppers and chili first reached China in the sixteenth century through contact with the European colonial powers, and spread rapidly. Today it is impossible to imagine Chinese food without them. The Sichuan peppercorn, also known as fagara or anise pepper, has been used far longer than any other type, and dates back to the time before the unification of the kingdom. The peppercorns should be roasted before use.

A whole array of other plant parts are also used for their sharp flavor, including garlic bulbs, the ginger rhizome, coriander leaves, and basil, the fruit of the star anise, mandarin peel, the flower bud of the clove, fennel seeds, mustard greens, and cassia. The fresh, dried, or blossom petals of the tiger lily, and day lily, known as "golden needles," are popular in Chinese vegetarian cooking. Many of the ingredients listed here were still unknown under the Han dynasty, and arrived in China later via Asiatic trade routes. Some products are still imported in large quantities today.

> Leeks and salt
> delicately seasoned
> [with ginger and Sichuan peppercorns],
> give a taste of harmony
> between the teeth.
>
> *Benxinzhai shushipu* (around 1250), chapter 1

Ready-made seasonings, such as the mixture known in the West as five-spice powder, which contains star anise, cassia, fennel, cloves, and Sichuan peppercorns, are used in many dishes. Monosodium glutamate, a crystalline powder that has no distinct taste of its own but enhances the flavor of other ingredients, is also extremely popular in Chinese

SPICES IMPORTED BY SEA, LISTED AMONG THE GOODS IN THE *ZHUFANZHI* (AROUND 1225)

Product	Description	Example of place of origin
Cloves	Buds of *Syzygium aromaticum*	Arabian peninsula
Nutmeg	Endosperm of *Myristica fragrans*	Moluccan Islands
Rosewater	Distilled petals of *Rosa* spp.	Arabian peninsula
Cardamom	Fruit of *Elettaria cardamomum*	Cambodia
Black peppercorns	Fruit of *Piper nigrum*	India
Cubeb peppercorns	Fruit of *Piper cubeba*	Java

cooking. However, medical experts disagree strongly about its effects, and it should be used with great care, if at all.

Aside from this, there are oils and condiments made from various substances whose spicy flavor often derives from a high proportion of preserved chilies, and pastes based on fermented beans. The best-known liquid condiment is undoubtedly soy sauce, which usually takes several months to produce. First, the boiled beans are fermented with added

Salt well (book illustration, 1637)

flour and brine; then the mixture is extracted and filtered several times over. Aside from quality and brand variety, there is a basic distinction between light and dark varieties of soy sauce; the latter contains added caramel. In earlier times the consistency and harvest date determined the sauce's appellation. The *Suiyuang shidan*, a cookbook from the year 1790, lists no fewer than seven distinct types.

Hoisin sauce, distinguished by a slightly sweet aroma, is made not from seafood, as the Chinese name *haixianjiang* suggests, but from various soy products combined with vinegar, sugar, and garlic. In addition, a number of liquid condiments are available based on fish, oysters, or crab. These generally exude a strong smell, sometimes almost odious for people unused to them. Vinegar, generally made from rice, gives food a sour taste, and is used particularly for preserving foodstuffs.

Two preserving agents were used for sweetening as well: honey, for which bees were already kept in ancient times, although on a rather small scale, and malt sugar, which was extracted from various cereals. It was during the Tang dynasty, under Indian influence, that the Chinese first started large-scale cultivation of sugar cane. Along with brown sugar they also produced refined sugar and invented quite poetic names for it like "sweet frost" and "stone honey."

Chapter Three

Fire, Ice, and Flavor

Conserving and Storing

Small farmers and tenants lived on the margin of subsistence for almost the whole imperial period. Cultivated fields were generally small, the soil quality moderate, harvests meager and storage possibilities limited. Moreover, cultivation was probably not diversified enough, with the resulting nutritional imbalances—but the sources reveal little about this, at least in ancient times. In contrast, there is much more information on the property-owning upper class. Manuals and guidebooks show that from the Han period onward, landed estates produced a wide variety of agricultural products and were largely self-sufficient.

Agricultural activity included soil cultivation and animal husbandry, production of alcoholic beverages, making of clothing and household objects, production of medicines, organization of the fuel supply, trade in seeds, duties in the local community, and participation in

Bronze tripod (eleventh century)

PICKLED VEGETABLES (SICHUAN)

Ingredients

1 small bok choy, cut into strips
1 large red pepper, cut into strips
2 large carrots, sliced
1 celery stalk, sliced
1 small radish, sliced
1 tbsp (50 g) thinly sliced ginger
2 tbsp dried chilies
1 tbsp roasted Sichuan pepper
5 star anise
2½ tbsp (30 g) sugar
¾ cup (150 g) salt
3 tbsp (40 ml) Kaoliang (sorghum liquor)

Preparation method

1. Combine the vegetables and distribute among containers with tight-fitting lids.
2. For the pickling liquid, bring around 2 L water to the boil in a pot.
3. Add the ginger, chilies, Sichuan pepper, star anise, sugar, salt, and Kaoliang, and simmer slowly until the sugar dissolves.
4. After cooling the liquid, pour over the vegetables and shut the containers tightly.
5. Store in a cool place for at least two days.

---

sacrificial rites. All these activities had to follow the rhythm of the four seasons. Storage and preservation of food, including such methods as drying, pickling, smoking, and curing, were especially important.

The agricultural system offered various possibilities for storing food-stuffs, ranging even on relatively small farms from the use of individual rooms to simple granary structures with no supporting walls between the foundations and the roof. Huge pottery jars and baskets, sometimes taller than a man, were also frequently used for storage.

In northern China, grain was already kept in storage pits in the fifth millennium B.C. This storing method, still used today in some regions, probably achieved its architectural peak under the Tang dynasty. The excavation of a storage complex built in Luoyang in the eighth century uncovered several hundred cellars reaching down to a maximum depth of 12 meters.

Pit storage is a good method for some cereals, particularly millet, but is unsuitable for rice because the grains start rotting very quickly. Anyway, in some parts of the country heavy rainfall makes underground storage impractical. As numerous clay miniatures from the Han period show, in southern China storage sheds were mostly built on pillars, with considerable space between the storeroom and the ground to protect the foods from damage by damp and flooding.

The buildings were generally supported by four to six pillars, some of which tapered toward the top and then thickened again to a truncated cone on the underside of the floor. This prevented animals from gaining access to the inside from underneath and eating away the stored grain, fruit, and vegetables. Cantilever beams were sometimes used to reinforce the floor of the building. In some cases, the platform, as well as the roof, had a circular form and was accessed by ladders made from planks with crosswise notches for steps.

Storage shed (book illustration, 1313)

See Appendix, Table 8.

Clay miniatures from the Han period, particularly in the Yellow River region, show multistoried storage sheds, some of which were tower-like complexes interconnected by covered passageways. These buildings were erected at ground level or on terraces, and their huge dimensions and elaborate details suggest that the imposing architecture was intended to demonstrate political power. Since ancient times the imperial court had always required an enormous amount of storage space. For example, in the twelfth century in Kaifeng, the capital of the Song dynasty, aside from innumerable grain stores there were big sheds exclusively for storing spices, milk products, tea, or alcohol.

Every year in the twelfth month the chief superintendent of the cold stores gives the order to cut ice. Then three times the required quantity is fetched and stored in the cellars. There, in spring, huge vessels are filled with food and drink that stay cool inside, waiting for use in sacrificial rites or at ceremonial banquets. . . . Finally in summer, public officials who have earned [special] merit receive the ice as a gift.

"Lingren" chapter in the *Zhouli* (second century B.C.)

Fruit vendor (propaganda poster, 1978)

However splendid the storage building, during the hot season meat spoils quickly if it has not been pickled, cured, smoked, or dried. This applies to a variety of other foods as well and is probably the main reason that cold stores were constructed in China, at least from the fifth century B.C. They consisted of well-insulated cellars and pits in which easily perishable products could be preserved by ice obtained in the winter.

Nowadays the majority of China's city dwellers own a refrigerator, and a quarter of all households in agricultural areas have refrigerating equipment. The proportion of fridge owners in farming villages has increased fivefold in the past fifteen years, although the figures still lag behind considerably in provinces less affected by industrial growth. Despite the environmental problems associated with rising production, and the seasonal shortages in energy supply, anybody traveling in China in the summertime heat can well understand the constant demand for refrigerators. Some firms have profited enormously from this, notably the Haier group, the world's biggest refrigerator manufacturer.

Canned foods are still a regular alternative. They have been available since the end of the nineteenth century, when factories in southern China adopted the process invented in Britain and began selling foods in closed, airtight tinplate containers. This meant that fish, in particular, could be hygienically packed and conserved for sale in regions far away from the coast. It was not long before consumers discovered the benefits of canned foods for traveling.

A Mirror of Life: The Markets

The demand for fresh food and conserves was enormous, particularly in the cities. In the Song metropolis Kaifeng at the beginning of the twelfth century, customers thronged the stalls and kiosks that occupied the streets or monastery courtyards from early morning until late evening, and sometimes all through the night. In many cases the produce was limited to a specific selection: For example, there was a special market for ginger, another for quail, and yet another for carp. Hawkers shouting their wares joined the competition for customers.

The biggest market [in Kaifeng] is [directly] outside the Donghua Gate [the eastern approach to the] imperial palace district. [The local residents] buy their supplies of food and drink there, including fresh seasonal produce such as flowers, fruit, fish, soft-shell turtles, shrimp and crab, along with quail and hare, and dried or cured meat."

Dongjing meng Hua lu (1148), chapter 1

Toward the end of the thirteenth century, Marco Polo claimed to have seen up to 50,000 traders at the regular food markets in Hangzhou selling goods they had brought with them. Even if he exaggerated the number, he was certainly describing a major organizational feat. The guilds were especially responsible for market organization. They had a fairly dense network of branches that provided accommodations for members and premises for arranging monetary transactions. Although these associations cultivated an image of equality, when it came to setting prices it was nearly impossible for individual merchants to ignore the wishes of the head of the guild, or of a small clique of guild bosses.

The tea guild [of Kaifeng] is dominated by more than ten members. They begin by ceremoniously playing host to the tea traders who travel to the capital, but go on to set such low prices that it is hardly worthwhile [for the traders to sell]. By selling the tea [bought cheaply in this manner] to ordinary members, they secure big profits for themselves. . . . All the other guilds presumably act in the same way.

Wang Anshi's petition to the throne, cited in *Xu zizhi tongjian changbian* (1072), chapter 236

Several centuries earlier, under the Tang dynasty, most business transactions were still under direct state control. The written sources do not correspond exactly to archeological finds, but at least they contain basic information on the typical architecture and organization of the commercial centers in the old Chinese capital, Chang'an. Although the staid Eastern Market was situated on the edge of the posh upper-class residential areas, it also bordered the entertainment district, whereas the cosmopolitan Western Market reflected the cultural diversity of merchants who came from the Silk Road. The two markets occupied a walled enclosure of almost 100 hectares, with an atmosphere like a bazaar, where every trade was allotted a fixed area (literally, "a row") for selling its products.

If inspection of equipment to measure volume, scales, and equipment to measure length reveals deviations from the standard, this should be punished in each case with 70 strokes. . . . Anybody who produces or sells goods made of unsuitable materials, or gives short measure, will be punished by 60 lashes. And if [the crime] leads to excessive profit it should be treated as a case of theft.

Tanglü shuyi (653), Article 26

The traders were principally permitted to sell their wares only at these markets, nowhere else, and were strictly supervised. Each market had a large administrative system answerable to the finance ministry. Its responsibilities included issuing licenses, certifying contracts, regularly setting prices, inspecting weights and measures, checking the money in circulation, supervising product quality, and keeping watch on visitors. The market authorities were even responsible for legal jurisdiction and

Large kitchen (stone relief, second century)

Watermelon vendor (watercolor, around 1870)

punishment in cases of minor infringements of the regulations, which were very strict.

Aside from commodity circulation, the government authorities were concerned with the resident service facilities on the market site, including offices, scriveners' shops, and undertakers. They kept an even sharper eye on the many pubs, teahouses, and hotels offering refreshment, accommodation, and entertainment. At the Eastern market the main task was to supervise the type of "service" available, as some young women were evidently prepared (although not officially licensed) to charm visitors with accomplishments other than singing or playing a musical instrument. Meanwhile, at the Western market the main sources of potential trouble were the crowds of foreigners, viewed anxiously by the authorities and regularly suspected of conspiracy.

There were also smaller markets in Chang'an, and food shops and restaurants in particular received permits to trade in city districts designated as purely residential. Occasionally the strict curfews were suspended, allowing nocturnal markets to be held. This created a special atmosphere in the city, where people mostly stopped moving around after nightfall.

At that time, Beijing was a sleepy, provincial town. This would change in the twelfth century, but it seems to have taken a while for

Sweet potato vendor (watercolor, around 1870)

When I was young it was difficult to find anything more [out of the ordinary] at the market in Beijing. There was only chicken, goat, mutton, and pork. Fish, on the other hand, was something special. Twenty years on, fish and crabs are now cheaper here than in the Yangzi area and the markets are full of scallops, noodlefish, razor clams, mussels, and prawns. No doubt about it: the southern lifestyle has [finally] reached the north.

Wu zazu (1602), chapter 9

its culinary arts to catch up with its political importance. The epicurean delights of southern Chinese cuisine were first discovered in the seventeenth century, when seafood actually replaced pork and mutton for a while. Later, under Manchu rule, meat and fowl returned to dominate menus, and fish reverted to being used again mainly in dried form.

Toward the end of the imperial age in Beijing, the grounds of temples and monasteries were popular places to purchase large quantities. Although the stalls were only open on certain days, the large number of markets meant that people could go shopping all year round. The stallholders normally had to sell their produce at much higher prices than the numerous hawkers who roamed the streets, but

FOOD PRICES IN BEIJING, 1839 (*GUANLUSI ZELI*)

	Copper coins (per piece)	Copper coins (per jin ["pound"])	Converted to kilograms (approx.)
Pig	2,500		
Pork		50	85
Pig's liver		27	46
Sheep	1,430		
Mutton		60	102
Goat	520		
Duck	360		
Chicken	120		
Rice		11	19
Wheat		10	17
Millet		9	15
White beans		9	15
Red beans		7	11
Ginger		46	78
Orange	50		
Apple	30		
Peach	20		
Plum	3		
Apricot	3		
Grapes		60	102

Note: At that time, workers in the city usually earned between 50 and 80 copper coins per day.

they offered the attraction of a much bigger selection. Aside from political guidelines, a series of other issues affected prices as well. In the case of grain, fruit, and vegetables, the main factors were the season, the quality of the goods, the harvest yield, transport overheads, and possible storage costs. Beijing was anything but cheap! Many products could be bought much cheaper in other regions.

In the countryside, too, markets were usually held on particular days of the month and followed a set rhythm. The scope could vary greatly. Whereas customers in prosperous regions found plenty on sale at markets with more than 1,000 stalls, in some places only the most important staple foods were available. Still, even the more leisurely markets had their unique charm.

Nowadays in big cities it is easier to get an overall picture of the number of markets where food is sold. The restrictions from the time of the Cultural Revolution—when private trading could bring

> [You can see] people laden with tea and salt, [along with] cackling hens and barking dogs. [Everything] is bartered: firewood for rice, [and] fish for alcohol.
> Here and there [you can spot] the green pennant signs of pubs where the old men sit,
> propped up and drowsy from [heavy] drinking.
>
> *Caochuang yunyu* (1274), chapter 4

harsh penalties—have long since been abolished, but the subsequent construction boom, in which entire city districts were demolished, has led to a reduction in public open space and thus, indirectly, to fewer markets. Customers in the twenty-first century buy mainly in stores. Those who can afford it shop in air-conditioned supermarkets, which may have less character but offer the benefit of hygienically packaged produce that stays fresh considerably longer on refrigerated shelves than on a chopping board surrounded by swarms of flies.

The Experts: Butchers and Cooks

In imperial China the market was not just a place to enjoy life; it was often a scene of horror as well. From ancient times it was used as a site for executions, which were usually staged as gruesome spectacles. The heads of executed people could frequently be seen on market grounds alongside the goods on sale, pub signs,

> Surrounded by fragrant aromas, the food vendors offer hot meals, stuffed pastries, and cakes. The pubs hang out their advertising banners; the tumblers and bowls are washed and polished to a shine. Finally, the butchers put out basins for the fat, and cut up pigs and sheep. Everything around them is heavily splattered with blood.
>
> *Liu Mengde ji* (808), chapter 25

Butchers (watercolor, around 1870)

and billboards. In this context, the occasional practice of slaughtering animals right next to snack food stalls seems less appalling, or at least more understandable.

As a rule, animals weren't treated very sensitively. The slaughtering process was predictably crude. Ancient wall paintings of slaughter scenes frequently portray men with cudgels, axes, or sledgehammers, although it is unclear whether the implements were used for stunning the animals or killing them. Another open question is whether the knives in the men's hands were used for bleeding the creatures to death or cutting them up. Butchers were usually not responsible for meat processing such as smoking or curing, and in any case, sausage production was of minor importance.

The butcher's trade was an explicitly male preserve for many centuries. The situation regarding food preparation was slightly more complicated because women do appear occasionally in depictions of kitchens found in tombs from the Han period. Most important, however, are the regional variations. Whereas written sources in the north of the country generally refer to men, women are often mentioned in the south, and not just servants but ladies of high rank.

> The pigs destined for slaughter arrived in the city [Kaifeng] through the Nanfeng Gate every day from morning until evening. None of them broke away, although the herds sometimes numbered over ten thousand animals with only a few drivers in charge. . . .
>
> Three to five men stand next to each other at the table, wield their knives, and joint the meat into big pieces, cut it into chunks or small strips, or pound it to suit the customer's wishes.
>
> *Dongjing meng Hua lu* (1148), chapters 2 and 4

The kitchen at court was certainly male-dominated, and its head could practically attain ministerial status. He was, after all, in command of a whole administration in which the tasks were divided among several large departments, each with its own hierarchy. Even if the *Zhouli*, written in the Han period, conveys an ideal rather than a realistic picture, its organizational chart is quite rational. It shows there were those who commanded large numbers of staff and who were responsible for slaughter, preparation, and serving. Even the servants in charge of the proper handling of meat broth, vinegar, and salt had twenty underlings each.

> Nowhere is negligence less excusable than in eating and drinking. Cooks are thoroughly uncouth fellows without any special talent who get careless right away if a day passes without praise or punishment. If you gobble up food that is not completely cooked, the next day it will be [served] in an even rawer state. If you are too polite to complain about a badly made broth, it will be cooked even more sloppily the next time. . . . The laziness of cooks and the indifference of diners are the biggest detriments in eating and drinking.
>
> *Suiyuan shidan* (1790), chapter 2

High standards were required, of course, especially with regard to adequate knowledge of the dietary rules that governed the choice and preparation of food. Successful cooking presumed familiarity with theoretical principles as well as plenty of practical experience, and a solid training was the way to ensure this. Talent was certainly admired, but creativity was not always appreciated. Perhaps one reason people started putting recipes in writing was to prevent excessive embellishing.

It is impossible to envisage Chinese cooking without noodles. They have a long tradition: no other country in the world can look back on a history of four thousand years of noodles. Interestingly, the earliest archeological find of noodles did not occur in the core regions with a reputation for inventiveness, but in the far western province of Qinghai.

Lamb and pork are really delicious, the five flavors are combined in mutual harmony, and beer is brewed from glutinous rice and ferment. Nonetheless, we can see a clear difference in quality if two persons [of differing ability] use the same ingredients in identical conditions for water, heat supply, outside temperature, and humidity. . . . In other words, even if the starting situations correlate, the results may not because they depend on the skill of the individual cook. . . .

In olden times, people took recipes seriously . . . [Today, however, there are cooks who] ignore the legacy of experience and claim they know anyway what the quality of beer and food is based on. They're casual about ingredients and careless with measurements. Convinced that [such trivial matters] are irrelevant, they rely entirely on their own ideas. The results are usually below par, and in most cases people spit them out again immediately after the first taste.

Yanguan dabeige ji (1075)

Researchers excavating a settlement there in 2005 found a clay bowl with surprising contents: thin noodles made from a millet-based flour, up to 50 centimeters long, and slightly resembling spaghetti. The find site, Lajia, has been famous ever since.

This does not mean that noodles have a continuous history dating back four thousand years, for the next evidence of noodle consumption is not until the Han dynasty. Yet the arguments for the existence of noodles in that period, which are based solely on written sources, are not entirely convincing. The term used for pasta at that time covered bakery products as well.

Through the ages, flour has always been the main basis of dough. Although products from ground wheat and rice grains have a larger market share today than in the past, flour produced from millet, buckwheat, and yams is also still used.

NOODLE PRODUCTION TECHNIQUES

Sliced noodles	*qiemian*	cut from folded pasta sheets with a knife; most widespread method	nationwide
Pulled noodles	*lamian*	increasing numbers of strands pulled with both hands and formed into threads; needs years of practice	northern China
Pressed noodles	*yamian*	pressed through a perforated container; like spaetzle, only longer	northeastern China
Thread noodles	*xianmian*	hand-formed, then hung on an expandable frame to pull them lengthways	southeastern China
Rope noodles	*suomian*	strands bundled by hand and pulled; relatively thick	northwestern China

Mung bean starch is used to make very fine glass noodles. Other ingredients may include salt, oil, baking soda, and various flavorings and colorings. Eggs have increasingly been used as well for approximately the last 500 years. Production methods for noodles vary greatly. There are at least five different techniques for achieving the right length and thinness.

There is also a long tradition in China of filled noodles resembling Italian varieties such as tortellini, ravioli and, most commonly, mezzalune. Written sources suggest they may date back as far as the Han dynasty, but the early records are not absolutely clear, and the oldest detailed description only dates back to the end of the third century. On the other hand, food remains excavated from a Tang period grave in Astana (Turfan Oasis) show that in the eighth century various forms of dumpling with different fillings were eaten in the northwestern border zones of the kingdom.

> Roll out the dough flat with a rolling pin, using pea flour to prevent sticking. Take care that the edges are not too thick. Then wrap the filling in the little rounds of dough.
>
> *Wu shi zhong kui lu* (13th century), chapter 1

In keeping with the many forms of noodles, and their possible fillings, many ways exist for their preparation. The main methods, aside from adding them to soups, are steaming, boiling, and frying. Different cooking processes can also be combined. Fried noodles, a standard ingredient of Chinese cooking, are usually steamed or boiled before they reach the pan. Sometimes this affects the terminology. The semicircular type of dumpling called *jiaozi*, for example, is known under three different names (*zheng-jiao, shuijiao, guotie*), depending on whether it is steamed, boiled, or fried. The term *wonton*, also known in the West, derives from an Anglicized version of the Cantonese pronunciation (*wonton*) of the terms *yuntun* ("cloud swallowing") and *huntun* (etymology unknown). The term *dimsum* has a similar derivation (*dimsam* =

Woman rolling out dough (clay figurine, eighth century)

DUMPLINGS (BEIJING AND SHANDONG)

Ingredients

1¾ cups (250 g) flour
1 cup of water
1lb (400 g) finely minced pork
1 tbsp finely chopped ginger
2 tbsp rice wine
1 head of bok choy with white center leaf ribs removed, cut into thin strips
2 tbsp soy sauce
2 tbsp sesame seed oil

Preparation method

1. Stir water slowly into the flour in a bowl, knead well, and let stand for at least half an hour.
2. Wrap the bok choy strips in a muslin cloth and press out the moisture.
3. Combine minced pork, bok choy, ginger, rice wine, soy sauce, and sesame oil, and mix well.
4. Shape the dough to a rope around 2–3 cm thick, then cut into slices around 1 cm thick and roll out into small rounds around 7–8 cm in diameter.
5. Put 1 teaspoon of filling in the middle of each disk, moisten the edges, fold into a semicircular shape, fold over the edges in some places and pinch together firmly.
6. Steam, boil, or fry; if frying is used, it should be done briskly, then liquid should be added. Cook in a closed pot until ready.

Note: The dumplings are generally eaten by dipping in a specially made seasoning mixture based on soy sauce and rice vinegar, which can be enriched with other ingredients such as sesame seed oil, garlic, or chili paste. Many Asian food stores sell frozen dough, which is much easier to use.

dianxin, or "tidbits"), but it has a broader semantic spectrum and covers other delicacies aside from filled pasta.

In prehistoric times the kings did not yet know of the transforming power of fire. They fed on the seeds of grasses and the fruit of trees. [This was supplemented by] the flesh of birds and beasts swallowed with skin and hair after drinking their blood. . . . Men only learned to use fire much later . . . and to fry, grill, boil, and roast.

"*Liyun*," chapter in the *Liji* (second century)

The Clean Cut: Kitchen Equipment

Raw food was not highly valued by gourmets in China. Even lettuce leaves were usually blanched before being arranged on plates or dishes. Fresh radishes and carrots were often carved artistically and seen mainly as decoration. Otherwise, most people regarded eating foods that were not cooked in some way—even very quickly—as "barbaric."

Hearthplaces can be identified in houses dating as far back as the Neolithic period. They were mostly simple hollows in the middle of the building encircled by raised earth or a low wall, and sometimes containing thick layers of ash. If reconstructions by architectural historians are correct, holes in the roof served as a chimney and were surrounded by a layer of clay to protect them from the fire. Stoves made of loam were common, at least by the Han period. The firebox had an opening for stoking at one end and a simple exhaust vent or a small flue tube at the other. The round-bottomed pots fitted exactly into circular cutouts in the stove lid. This was the standard construction principle for many centuries.

Until well into the twentieth century, cooking stoves were usually fired with wood, charcoal, coal, dung, and straw. Kerosene was sometimes used in the cities but was a minor fuel compared with gas in recent times. Standard electric cookers are still not a serious alternative: the traditional cooking vessels, with their rounded bottoms, are not really suitable for flat hotplates, and the slow, complicated temperature control of electric stoves is another drawback.

Again, in the Neolithic period cooks were already using a container with a perforated bottom placed in a bigger pot with boiling water. These steamers were initially made of clay, but bronze was used as well from the Shang dynasty

Cook and servant (thirteenth century)

Bronze steamer (second century B.C.)

onward. Today they are mainly made of bamboo and aluminum. This basically gentle way of preparing food has survived up to the present and is still popular for cooking rice, despite the wider use of more efficient electrical devices for maintaining constant heat and regulating cooking time. There are also very early records of people using bowls or basins to heat fuel—usually charcoal—to red hot, and grilling meat over them.

> The transformation processes that occur [during cooking] in the tripod pot are just as complex, and nearly as mysterious, as the art of archery, the skill in steering a wagon, the interplay of yin and yang, and the passage of the seasons.
>
> *Lüshi Chunqiu* (around 240 B.C.), chapter 14

Terms in kitchen technology are often difficult to deal with because meanings have shifted over time. It is therefore always important to look at the historical as well as the regional context when undertaking a translation. Moreover, stark semantic differentiation contrasts with the development of innumerable synonyms, making it nearly impossible to express terms consistently and understandably. Naturally, this is relevant to describing the various types of food preparation as well.

Unfortunately, we can no longer identify the exact moment when people began heating food in fat. However, edible oil from a vegetable base seems to have been widespread by the Tang period at the latest. It was initially made from hemp seed, rapeseed, and turnips. Yet there is evidence that tallow from cows, pigs, sheep, and dogs was already in use several centuries earlier; the sources emphasize the importance of finding the optimal combination of rendered animal fat and meat type. Today the use of animal fat is confined to specific regions; it is used not for frying but for flavoring at the end of cooking. The earliest description of starch production dates back to the sixth century. Before then, liquids were thickened mainly with crumbled grains of rice and millet.

In the course of history, pots were made from a very wide variety of materials. One particular material dominated until the twentieth century, at least among the majority of the population: clay. As far back as the Neolithic period, this involved complex technology. A significant development was the tempering done by adding sand (to make the pots able to withstand higher temperatures) and straw (for improved flexibility in molding). The potter's wheel, which appeared before the third millennium B.C., helped to standardize the forms and speed up production. The quality of kilns also improved gradually, making it possible to produce glazed stoneware from the Shang dynasty onward.

BRAISED PORK BELLY

Ingredients

1 lb (500 g) pork belly
1 tbsp peanut oil
2 tbsp sugar
3 tbsp rice wine
1 tbsp sliced ginger
1 tbsp sliced garlic
1 star anise
5 dried chilies
1 small piece of Ceylon cinnamon, or half a cinnamon stick

Preparation method

1. Simmer the meat in boiling water for several minutes.
2. Heat the oil and caramelize the sugar in it.
3. Add the meat (already cut into cubes of around 3 cm), and the rice wine.
4. Add just enough water to cover the meat.
5. Add ginger, garlic, star anise, chilies and cinnamon.
6. Bring to the boil and leave to simmer for 1 hour.
7. Remove the meat (without the spices) and season to taste with salt and sugar.

Note: There are countless variations on this dish, which is usually served on a bed of vegetables. It was reputed to be Mao Zedong's favorite meal. Soy sauce can also be used for seasoning (although the "Great Chairman" is supposed to have turned his nose up at this).

Achieving higher temperatures was also a precondition for casting metal, so it is hardly surprising that the quality and quantity of bronze vessel production first peaked at around the same time. However, use of bronze was initially restricted to royal household circles and was used only for rituals. Perhaps this was fortunate for less-well-off people, because aside from copper and zinc, the alloys often had a relatively high lead content, which was not necessarily good for health.

The sheer weight of the objects, which were cast with the help of clay molds, meant they were unlikely to be found in everyday use; some vessels weighed far more than their owners. Although pots and bowls were increasingly used for profane purposes in the first century B.C., and the decoration was considerably modified, the basic models for pottery, which nearly all dated back to the Neolithic age, remained astonishingly unchanged.

SELECTED COOKING METHODS

Frying	pan frying briskly in shallow oil	*jian*
	pan frying in shallow oil, stirring constantly ("stir-fry")	*chao*
	pan frying very quickly after cooking	*bao*
Grilling	heating by radiant dry heat	*kao*
Deep frying	frying or deep immersion in hot oil	*zha*
Ember roasting	cooking in open fire or hot embers	*wei*
Clay baking	cooking by wrapping in moist clay	*baozai*
Braising /stewing	brief frying, then cooking in liquid	*ao, men, peng, shao*
Boiling	generally: cooking in liquid	*gun, peng, zhu*
	cooking in stock	*lu*
	cooking in liquid at the table	*shuan*
	cooking by repeated boiling	*chuan*
Blanching	brief scalding, then steeping	*dun, qin*
Simmering	cooking at a gentle bubble	*dao, wei*
Poaching	cooking in liquid below boiling point	*cuan, zhuo*
Stewing /braising	cooking in a small quantity of liquid	*jue, wen*
Steaming	cooking in water vapor	*zheng*

Now my knife has been in use for nineteen years; it has cut up several thousand oxen, and yet its edge is as sharp as if it had newly come from the whetstone. There are the interstices of the joints, and the edge of the knife has no (appreciable) thickness; when that which is so thin enters where the interstice is, how easily it moves along! The blade has more than room enough. Nevertheless, whenever I come to a complicated joint, and see that there will be some difficulty, I proceed anxiously and with caution, not allowing my eyes to wander from the place, and moving my hand slowly. Then by a very slight movement of the knife, the part is quickly separated, and drops like [a clod of] earth to the ground. Then standing up with the knife in my hand, I look all round, and in a leisurely manner, with an air of satisfaction, wipe it clean, and put it in its sheath.

Zhuangzi (third century B.C.), chapter 3. Translated by James Legge. Oxford University Press, 1885

Online: Chapter 3:2; http://oaks.nvg.org/zhuangzi1-.html#3

Iron utensils became increasingly important for preparing food from the third century B.C. onward. The Chinese utilized the potential of the casting process to make cookware long before the technology arrived in Europe. The early forms of the wok, a deep concave pan, may have been developed at that time. The word *wok*, which derives from the Cantonese pronunciation of the word *pot* (*guo*), has now become common in the West.

A cutting tool in good working order is by far the most important appliance for butchers and cooks. Knives, on the other hand, were shaped by forging. The blades were sometimes of steel and could be very sharp. The kitchen cleaver in particular has a large variety of uses, from chopping up bones to producing wafer-thin slices and finely chopped masses. The broad blade allows the user to pound meat, crush gar-

Clay bowl with portable warmer (fourth century B.C.)

lic or ginger, and lift ingredients directly into the pot. Another standard kitchen fixture is a massive block of wood as a work surface for cutting up meat and vegetables. Particularly for stir-frying, it is essential to cut the food into small pieces so that the heat reaches them more easily and they cook very quickly.

There is a whole series of utensils with a long tradition dating back to ancient times. Way back then, herbs and spices were already ground with a pestle and mortar, and there is even archaeological evidence of ginger graters, as well as skewers and long-handled forks used for grilling and frying, and ladles for serving broths and other foods. On the other hand, it is hard to find evidence in antiquity for the wok spatula, an indispensable utensil in modern-day Chinese kitchens,

> If too much is fried [at once] the heat cannot reach its [full] power and the meat will not get crisp. Consequently, one should not use more than half a pound of meat and, for chicken and fish, only six ounces at most. If that is not enough, it is better to wait until everything has been eaten up and then repeat [the cooking]. When boiling, however, one should use the largest possible quantities, because meat weighing under twenty pounds turns out relatively tasteless.
>
> *Suiyuan shidan* (1790), chapter 1

especially for cooking strips of meat, and for the skimmer with its basketlike wire mesh that offers a convenient way to remove and drain boiled or fried foods after cooking.

Nutritional scientists and doctors would obviously agree that cleanliness has top priority in the kitchen. But it is important to avoid the mistake of linking maintenance of good hygiene directly with the quality of the gastronomic experience. Worrying about hygienic standards can seriously reduce the pleasure of eating and drinking in China. If you want to enjoy a meal to the full, it is generally advisable to leave out a visit to the kitchen.

As we have mentioned, most foods in China are cooked. The Chinese often preserve the few uncooked foods by pickling them in alcohol, vinegar, honey, or syrup. Sometimes they do this with live creatures, particularly seafood. They are certainly not squeamish about handling "fresh foods." Hawkers often sell live fish by carrying them from one restaurant to another in plastic bags containing very little water.

LEMON CHICKEN (GUANGDONG)

Ingredients

10 oz (300 g) boned chicken breast cut into strips
1 tsp salt
3 tbsp cornstarch
3 tbsp peanut oil
3 tbsp sugar
1 tbsp rice vinegar
1 large unsprayed lemon, one half thinly sliced, one half squeezed for juice
1 tbsp cornstarch dissolved in 2 tbsp cold water
2 tbsp chopped parsley

Preparation method

1. Salt the meat and rub with the cornstarch.
2. Stir-fry the chicken strips in oil at high heat, stirring constantly.
3. Pour off the oil if necessary, leaving only a thin layer in the pan; keep the meat warm on a serving plate.
4. Heat the lemon slices, sugar, vinegar, and lemon juice in the remaining oil.
5. As soon as the sugar is dissolved, add the cornstarch solution and cook until thickened.
6. Pour the sauce over the chicken.
7. Decorate the dish with the lemon slices, sprinkle with parsley, and serve immediately.

Above: ceramic bowl (ninth century); *below*: gold bowl (eighth century)

Feasting the Eyes: The Tableware

The old adage that we eat with our eyes as well as our stomachs is entirely applicable for Chinese food. Although the aesthetic aspect of food culture is less predominant than in Japan, decorative elements are indispensable, at least for festive meals, particularly in relation to the composition of the dishes, artistic vegetable carving, and choice of tableware.

Pottery has been the main material for plates, bowls, and dishes from the Neolithic age to the present day. Starting from the Han period, the outer layer of ceramic ware was often coated with a slip, or glaze. The pottery with polychrome lead glaze known as *sancai* ("three colors") is particularly renowned and was found in large quantities in Tang dynasty tombs. This is also the era of the first known specimens of porcelain, a translucent white ceramic material with high kaolin content and hard, clinking shards. In the Tang period only the elite used it. Records show that the imperial household owned a particularly costly type called *mise* ("secret color"). Ceramic art first reached its peak under the Song dynasty in a unique, harmonious combination of elegantly simple forms and restrained coloring that was never repeated.

> The porcelain from Dayi
> is both light and hard.
> People here say,
> when you tap it, the sound
> is like the plaintive clinking of jade.
> Hoar frost and snow do not attain
> the whiteness of your bowls.
>
> *You yu Wei Chu qi Dayi ciwan (756)*

Looking at the bronze objects discovered in archaeological excavations, it is not always easy to differentiate between the pots for preparing food and drink and the serving dishes. We should note, however, that in arranging food for the table the traditional links with religious rites were gradually forgotten, and food vessels were used mainly for secular purposes. After the founding of the empire, large quantities of bronze tableware were produced, but the quality seldom achieved that of the peak period.

Lacquer ware also attracted increasing attention at around the same time. Initially used to embellish other materials, it went into mass production in the Han period. It was produced especially in the imperial manufactories that employed highly specialized artisans, each responsible for a specific step in the production process, starting with making the core (usually from softwood or textile fibers), then applying several layers of lacquer, and finally painting the decoration on the finished

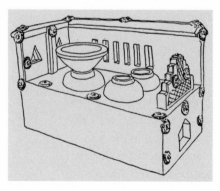

Cooking stove (clay miniature, second century)

object. A particularly elaborate construction process involved leaving lacquer-soaked hemp cloths to dry out to a stiff, modeled, free-standing form. Despite the large number of pieces produced, lacquer objects remained luxury goods, as they were much more expensive than the equivalent bronze ware. In fact, lacquer goods have never lost their special value, but such attractive pieces were rarely made later, at least not for regular use in eating and drinking.

The chronology for silver and gold design was quite a different story. Processing of these precious metals dated back
many centuries, but their use in tableware
production first became really important
in the Tang period. An unmistakable foreign influence can be detected here, even

Raw gold and jade should not be processed to [produce] tableware for public
officials below the first rank. Moreover,
raw silver should not be used below the
sixth rank.

Decree from the year 706, cited in the *Tang huiyao*
(961), chapter 31

though the number of imported pieces declined rapidly and the orna-
mentation was increasingly adapted to the imperial court's taste. The silver plates, bowls, jugs, and cups with decoration highlighted by gilding
are particularly impressive. The Tang dynasty also produced the earliest
examples of cloisonné (enamel decoration) that have been discovered.

Finally, there was heightened interest in glassware under the Tang,
although it never had a genuine boom because the most valuable objects
still came from abroad. The major finds date back to the excavations in
the Famen monastery. Among the discoveries in this monastery complex, which was built around 120 kilometers to the west of the then capital, Chang'an, was a set of dark blue plates decorated with etched flower
motifs. The costly pieces were probably imported from the Near East or
Middle East. In the year 874, Emperor Xizong personally ordered them
to be deposited, together with Buddhist reliquaries, in the underground
palace built beneath the pagoda.

The use of chopsticks is a keynote of Chinese cooking and eating.
The oldest archaeological evidence for them so far is a pair cast in bronze
found in Tomb 1005 at Houjiazhuang, not far from the Shang capital,
Anyang, and dated to the thirteenth or twelfth century B.C. This does
not mean, however, that a tradition of using chopsticks had already been
established back then, or perhaps even earlier, and survived until the
present as a standard, universal practice. If we are to believe compendia
of rites compiled under the Han dynasty, there was still a lengthy period in which specific dishes, including rice, were eaten with the hands.
Decoration aside, chopsticks are made from an extremely wide variety of
materials, ranging from wood and bamboo for everyday use to lacquer,
ivory, silver, gold, and jade for upper-class banquets. Plastic and stainless
steel have been increasingly used since the twentieth century.

Spoons, spatulas, and ladles have an unbroken, well-documented history. Exquisite lacquer objects have survived, particularly from the Han
period; utensils made of gold and silver came later. As with chopsticks,
which were used in a variety of ways, simpler kinds of cutlery were used

not just for serving and eating, but also for cooking at the stove. For a long time that was the only function of knives and forks, or so it seems from the large numbers of archeological finds and the interpretation of the images they contain. European cutlery first became popular in the cities in the second half of the nineteenth century, with the emergence of a growing number of Western-style restaurants frequented not only by foreigners but also by wealthy Chinese customers.

Chapter Four

A Culinary Cosmos

Landscapes, Climates, and Contrasts

China today covers an area of more than 9.6 million square kilometers, roughly the same size as the total territory of the United States. In such a vast country there are great variations in types of landscape, climatic zones, and vegetation. This inevitably affects the development of specific cultural features, and the culinary diversity.

To the west, the country is protected by high mountains, including Tianshan, Kunlun, Karakorum, and the Himalayas, with a series of peaks at 7,000 and 8,000 meters. The mountain ranges are not insurmountable, although the passes are covered with ice and snow for many months of the year. Under these conditions, it is remarkable that there has been a continuous, intensive interchange of goods and ideas through the ages—as shown, above all, by the long historical success story of the Silk Road. Although part of the Turfan Basin forms the world's second-deepest geological depression (at 154 meters below sea level), China is not generally a country of lowlands. Only 14 percent of the total territory consists of zones under 500 meters above sea level, whereas 33 percent comprises highlands above 2,000 meters. At least one third of the country is covered with hill ranges up to 1,000 to 2,000 meters high.

> I came to the mountains to collect ferns. Now it is evening, and hunger is tormenting me. The valleys are filled with wind and storms, and my clothes are damp from hoar frost and dew. All around, pheasants are calling and monkeys frolicking. When I look homeward, I lose heart.
>
> *Shanzaixing* (around 210)

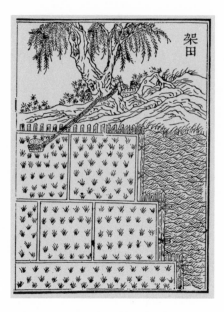

架
田

Irrigation (book illustration, 1742)

Nearly as impassable as the mountains are the regions where drought and desertification have caused severe water shortage and permanent damage to the plant cover. Many plateaus, basins, and depressions are arid or semiarid, part of a dry belt extending as far as North Africa and including the Gobi, the world's second largest desert. Here, as in the Taklamakan, survival is only possible within a network of oases. At least dry grass and bushes grow in the steppe regions, allowing cattle farming over wide areas. The different forms of animal husbandry, from transhumance to nomadism, necessitate the changing of pastures in a fixed, seasonal rhythm that determines not only the yearly calendar, but also the political and social structures.

Numerous rivers flow through the country like arteries. The most important are the Yangzi (6,300 kilometers or 3,900 miles long) and the Huanghe, the "Yellow River" (5,464 kilometers or 3,395 miles long). Far from being obstacles, like many other rivers they function as communication channels, bringing people and cultures closer together. They are also essential for irrigation; but they can be an enormous threat, because they flood repeatedly, causing devastation.

> There are no birds to be seen in the sky, and no animals on the ground. However hard you look in every possible direction for the way through, you won't find it. The only signposts are the dried-out bones of the dead.
>
> *Foguoji* (around 420), chapter 1

The coastal strip bordering the country to the east, particularly the section north of the Yangzi estuary, forms a clear boundary, and the Chinese people regarded it as such for many centuries, but they only seem to have become aware of the neighboring island world in the south later on. Although there are relatively early records of maritime contact with various Asian regions, it was mainly foreign seafarers who initiated organized trade relations. China only became a serious maritime power for a short period in the fifteenth century.

The diversity of landscape types is mirrored by the climatic contrasts. Whereas monsoon winds determine the seasonal rhythms of the coastal

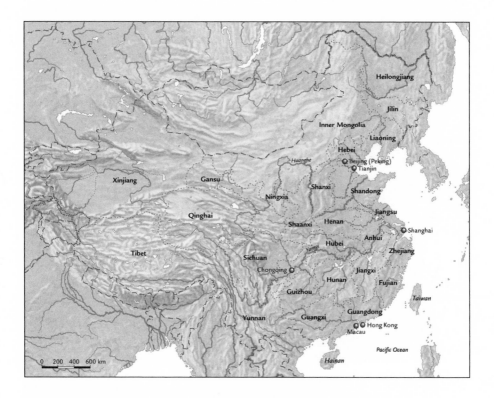

China today

region, continental air masses from the west dominate parts of the interior. We can broadly identify at least three major zones—from the south to the north—characterized by tropical, subtropical, and moderate climates. There are correspondingly big regional variations in temperature and precipitation.

The climatic conditions and specific features of the natural environment decisively affect agricultural productivity. According to reliable estimates, a maximum of 12 to 13 percent of China's total territory can be used for farming, and only a small proportion of this is high-yield land. The Sichuan basin and the lowlands, which are dominated by the lower reaches of the Huanghe and Yangzi rivers, yield particularly rich harvests. Between the two rivers is a horizontal divide between the mainly wheat-growing areas and those where rice is the primary crop.

Given that poor terrain often coincides with sparse population, the production statistics are not necessarily reliable. Still, they do indicate

Arable farming (painted tile, third century)

how limited the agricultural resources are, and how dramatic the effects of drought and flooding can be. In the past, even official historiography, which tended to paint a rosy picture, was obliged to record natural disasters, famines, and epidemics year after year.

The loess region in the lower reaches of the Huanghe was traditionally regarded as China's original cultural nucleus, but this no longer applies. Archeological finds from supposedly peripheral areas show that highly individual traditions were nurtured in many parts of the country. In the long term they contributed material and intellectual stimuli that played their part in developing the characteristics we associate today with the Han, the largest ethnic group in the population.

Regional Cooking

Natural constants have a fairly strong influence on the cooking traditions of the various regions. Coastal areas and river valleys clearly offer different resources from mountain regions or steppes, for example. Also very important is whether farming is possible for nearly the whole year or restricted to a period of a little more than three months. The boundaries between individual landscapes, climatic areas and vegetation zones matter much less and only have a limited effect on the differences between various regional cuisines.

THE EAST

The area of the lower reaches and estuary of the Yangzi has been a nucleus of Chinese civilization since ancient times. Although the megacity Shanghai, today's regional center, can boast a long history, it only achieved world ranking under the influence of European colonial rule. Before then, other cities—including the former capitals, Hangzhou and Nanjing—were much more important. Aside from Shanghai, the core areas of regional cooking are the coastal provinces Jiangsu and Zhejiang, but the regional influence continues further inland as far as Anhui and Jiangxi.

Since Buddhism was an influential part of the culture that grew up at the East China Sea, vegetarian dishes are particularly prominent. Otherwise the menu is dominated by fish and seafood served in a wide variety of ways. The province of Fujian is a special case: There, autochthonous traditions and conventions from the neighboring provinces, Zhejiang and Guangdong, have combined to create a highly individual style of cuisine in which soups are an essential part of a proper meal.

FRIED FISH (JIANGSU)

Ingredients

1 whole fish (e.g., porgy, 2–3 lb [1,000–1,200 g])
⅓ cup (50 g) flour
½ oz (15 g) dried shiitake mushrooms (soak in warm water for 30 minutes, then remove stalks and cut into thin strips)
1 tbsp chopped ginger
3 finely chopped scallions
2 oz (50 g) bamboo shoots, cut into thin strips
1 carrot, scraped and cut into strips
A generous measure of peanut oil
2 tbsp cornstarch, dissolved in 4 tbsp cold water
Sauce blend from ½ cup (⅛ L) chicken stock and 2 tbsp each of soy sauce, rice wine, and sugar

Preparation method

1. Wash the fish under cold water; cut off the head, and loosen the backbone and frame so that the two fillets are only attached at the tail fin.
2. Score the fillets in a crosshatch pattern and dust them well with flour.
3. Fry the fish in plenty of oil until golden brown; drain, and keep warm.
4. Stir-fry mushrooms, ginger, scallions, bamboo shoots, and carrots in 2 tbsp oil.
5. Add the sauce blend and bring to the boil.
6. Thicken with the cornstarch solution.
7. Pour the sauce over the fish and serve immediately.

Note: You can dust the fish head with flour, fry it together with the fish, and arrange all the pieces on the platter to look like a whole fish. The common name for this dish is "squirrel-fish" because the fillets curl into squirrel-tail shapes during frying.

THE SOUTH

In the year 111 B.C., the imperial troops succeeded in conquering the city of Panyu in the Pearl River (Zhujiang) delta. Panyu, the center of a kingdom that had been largely independent until then, was the nucleus of today's Canton (Guangzhou). The conquerors found a courtly lifestyle that could well compare with the refined atmosphere of central China's palaces. Abundant finds of vessels for cooking, eating, and drinking from the tomb of a monarch buried not far from the residence twelve years earlier indicate a high level of epicurean culture as well. It is not clear what was served in these vessels, but the existence of the nearby port and the import of exotic merchandise suggest a cosmopolitan atmosphere that would certainly have influenced the menu.

Records from later ages testify at least to an impressive variety of flavors. This is hardly surprising when we consider that countless spices from overseas first reached China through the "southern gates" of the kingdom. Yet some foods sold at Cantonese markets—including dog, cat, monkey, and rat—often seemed alien, and sometimes disgusting, to people from outside the provinces of Guangdong and Guangxi, and this still applies today. At the same time, the region is widely renowned and appreciated for its sophisticated approach to fish and seafood, its great selection of fruits and vegetables, and its perfect method of preparing rice.

SWEET AND SOUR PORK (CANTON)

Ingredients

1½ lb (750 g) pork fillet, diced into half-inch (1.5 cm) cubes
Salt
1 beaten egg
Mixture of 2 tbsp flour and 2 tbsp cornstarch
A generous measure of peanut oil
1 red pepper, diced into half-inch (1.5-cm) pieces
Sauce blend made of ½ cup (⅛ L) chicken stock, 3 tbsp rice vinegar, 1 tbsp soy sauce, and 6 tbsp sugar
1 tbsp cornstarch dissolved in 2 tbsp water

Preparation

1. Salt the meat and put in a dish with the beaten egg.
2. Add the combined flour and cornstarch, and mix well.
3. Cook the pork pieces in plenty of oil until they are golden brown and crispy; drain, and keep warm.
4. Fry the red pepper quickly in 2 tbsp oil.
5. Add the sauce blend and bring to the boil.
6. As soon as the sugar dissolves, add the cornstarch solution and stir to thicken.
7. Remove from the heat, pour over the meat, and serve immediately.

THE NORTH

Beijing was the seat of the royal court almost continuously under the last three dynasties: the Mongolian Yuan, the Chinese Ming, and the Manchurian Qing. This undoubtedly affected the diversity and quality of the cuisine, because the cooking style from Shandong had previously dominated in the lower reaches of the Huanghe. Even today, residents of the Shandong peninsula try to claim culinary hegemony in relation to the capital and the provinces of Hebei, Henan, Shanxi, and Shaanxi.

In the past, few people could afford exquisite care and artistry when selecting ingredients and preparing food. The majority of the population had to live relatively modestly, mostly on wheat and millet products eaten in the form of noodles, dumplings, and bread. Fresh fruit and vegetables seemed almost a luxury, particularly in winter. Meat was hardly ever served. The long cold period is perhaps also the reason why the Beijing region was known for more ingenious preservation methods than the rest of the country—especially pickling, curing, and drying. Seasonings were probably plain and simple, and garlic, ginger, sesame oil, and soy sauce provided most of the flavorings.

HOT AND SOUR SOUP (BEIJING)

Ingredients

4 cups (1 L) strong chicken stock
4 oz (100 g) pork, cut into thin strips
2 oz (50 g) bamboo shoots, cut into thin strips
1 oz (25 g) dried shiitake mushrooms: soak for 30 minutes in warm water, then remove the stalks and cut into thin strips
2 oz (50 g) clotted pig's blood
3.5 oz (100 g) bean curd, diced small
2 tbsp soy sauce
2 tbsp rice vinegar
1 tsp salt
½ tsp ground white pepper
2 tbsp cornstarch dissolved in 4 tbsp cold stock
1 beaten egg
2 chopped scallions

Preparation method

1. Bring the pork fillet, bamboo shoots, and shiitake to the boil in the stock, then turn down the heat and simmer for a few minutes.
2. Add the bean curd, pig's blood, and all the seasonings, and bring to the boil again.
3. Thicken with the cornstarch solution.
4. Beat the egg in until it starts to curdle, then quickly remove the soup from the heat.
5. Sprinkle with the scallions.

Note: The pig's blood is optional and can be omitted.

THE WEST

The center of this region is the fertile Red Basin. The conquest by troops of the royal house of Qin failed to end the region's political independence completely: Sichuan's history has been deeply affected by struggles for autonomy and recurrent rebellions. This is enhanced by a strong awareness of cultural individuality that has survived up to the present day. In neighboring Hunan province, too, long after the unification of the empire it seems clear that some unusual traditions for central China have persisted. The inhabitants of both these provinces have one special thing in common: their fondness for spicy food.

This was not necessarily always the case. Pepper was a costly imported product for a long time, and chilies, which tend to dominate the taste of Sichuan dishes today, first reached China in the sixteenth century, along with sweet peppers. Before then, as we know from burial finds from the Han period, the main seasoning was Sichuan pepper. It has a slightly numbing effect on the tongue and gums, but is not as hot as chili, and leaves a lingering taste rather like lemon or anise, depending on the type. Some kinds of food preparation indigenous to Yunnan, Guizhou, and Hubei can be classified as western Chinese cooking, but the dishes in those provinces are generally milder.

SPICY CHICKEN (SICHUAN)

Ingredients

10 oz (300 g) chicken breast, diced (max. ½ inch × ½ inch [1.5 × 1.5 cm])
1 tsp salt
2 tbsp cornstarch
2 tbsp dried chilies
2 tbsp lard
6 scallions, white parts chopped into 3 cm pieces
3 tbsp soy sauce
1 tbsp vinegar
1 tsp sugar
3 tbsp rice wine
½ cup (100 ml) chicken stock
2 oz (50 g) dry-roasted cashew nuts
1 tbsp roasted Sichuan pepper

Preparation method

1. Salt the meat and rub with the cornstarch.
2. Fry the diced meat and chilies in the lard at a very high temperature, stirring constantly.
3. Remove the chilies.
4. Stir in the scallions and fry together.
5. Add the mixture of soy sauce, vinegar, sugar, rice wine, and chicken stock, and bring to the boil.
6. Stir in the cashew nuts, and season with Sichuan pepper.

Consequently, there are many possible variations when trying to classify China from a culinary perspective. One very popular version—using the highly symbolic number 8—is based on eight provinces: Sichuan, Hunan, Guangdong, Shandong, Jiangsu, Anhui, Fujian, and Zhejiang. The model probably most easily understood in the West is based on the compass points and is limited to four core areas: Shanghai (east), Canton (south), Sichuan (west), and Beijing (north). This means that each of these territories contains great diversity, but at least we get a rough outline picture. The northern periphery, covering the area from the Taklamakan to the Amur, is usually ignored in discussions of culinary culture.

In addition, the four major regions are associated with four distinct flavors: the cuisine in the east is sour; in the south, sweet; in the west, spicy; and in the north, salty. This is very simplified, of course, because the migration dictated by individual needs or governmental pressure led to regular cultural exchange and career-based mobility of public officials, soldiers, and merchants. Since this inevitably had an effect on culinary variations, differences in cooking styles based on the cardinal points and administrative entities can only be a rough guide.

Rich Man, Poor Man . . .

In 1972–1973 three graves were uncovered in Mawangdui, a suburb of Changsha in Hunan province. They were presumed to be the last resting place of the marquis of Dai, who died in 186 B.C., and two of his close relatives. One of them, a woman of around fifty years old, was buried around twenty years later, and most archeologists and historians think she was the nobleman's widow.

The lady's high rank can be seen from the fact that there were massive wooden shelves with multiple nested coffins built into the 16-meter-deep pit of Tomb 1. The find is notable for the outstanding quality of the burial objects, which numbered more than 1,000 and gave a good illustration of upper-class living standards. They included foodstuffs deposited in thirty bamboo containers, in numerous lacquer and pottery vessels, and in a series of hemp sacks. The foods were subjected to thorough botanical and zoological analysis.

Moreover, the inscriptions on the wooden tags noting the content of the boxes, and the grave inventory details written on 312 small bamboo tablets, allow other ingredients (including bamboo shoots, taro, quail, and wild geese) to be approximately identified. They also mention an assortment of dishes, including "fried dog's liver," "dried beef," "minced lamb," and "fish and lotus root stew."

This discovery is also useful for reconstructing different preparation methods—frying, deep-frying, braising, boiling, and steaming—and several processes for seasoning and preserving. The products seem to have been pickled in preserving agents including soy sauce, vinegar and honey, or were salted and sugared, dried and cured. Finally, the beverages included a selection of beers based on millet, rice, and wheat.

The remains in Tomb 1 at Mawangdui give a glimpse of the culinary diversity enjoyed by the Chinese upper class. They also give an idea of the quantities that were sometimes consumed. The rather plump lady who was buried here obviously made little effort to control her appetite. Analysis of her stomach contents revealed that just before she died she had eaten a substantial pile of melon seeds. Her eating habits are quite likely to have contributed to her arteriosclerosis and the fact she suffered from coronary thrombosis.

Indeed, overeating was one of the privileges that distinguished the elites of the Tang period from the mass of the population. It is particu-

VEGETABLE FOODS AND SPICES FROM TOMB 1 AT MAWANGDUI

Grains	Rice	*Oryza sativa*	grains
	Wheat	*Triticum turgidum*	grains
	Barley	*Hordeum vulgare*	grains
	Common millet	*Panicum miliaceum*	grains
	Foxtail millet	*Setaria italica*	grains
Pulses	Soybean	*Glycine max*	seeds
	Azuki bean	*Vigna angularis*	seeds
Root vegetables	Indian lotus	*Nelumbo nucifera*	rhizome
Fruits	Jujube	*Ziziphus jujuba*	fruit
	Common melon	*Cucumis melo*	seeds
	Chinese pear	*Pyrus pyrifolia*	fruit
	Japanese flowering apricot	*Prunus mume*	fruit
Seeds and spices	Mustard	*Brassica cernua*	seeds
	Chinese mallow	*Malva verticillata*	seeds
	Hemp	*Cannabis sativa*	seeds
	Sichuan pepper	*Zanthoxylum piperitum*	fruit
	Zhejiang camphor	*Cinnamomum chekiangensis*	bark
	Buffalo grass	*Hierochloe odorata*	rhizome
	Lesser galangal	*Alpinia officinarum*	rhizome

ANIMAL FOODS IDENTIFIED FROM TOMB 1 AT MAWANGDUI

Fish	Common carp	*Cyprinus carpio*
	Crucian carp	*Carassius auratus*
	Yellowcheek	*Elopichthys bambusa*
	Chinese carp	*Acanthobrama simoni*
	Freshwater yellowfin	*Xenocypris argentea*
	Mandarin fish	*Siniperca sp.*
Breeding cattle and game animals	Domestic pig	*Sus scrofa domestica*
	Cattle	*Bos taurus domesticus*
	Domestic sheep	*Ovis ammon aries*
	Domestic dog	*Canis lupus familiaris*
	Japanese deer	*Cervus nippon*
	Chinese hare	*Lepus sinensis*
Fowl and winged game	Goose	*Anser sp.*
	Mandarin duck	*Aix galericulata*
	Duck	*Anas sp.*
	Chicken	*Gallus gallus domesticus*
	Bamboo partridge	*Bambusicola thoracica*
	Common pheasant	*Phasianus colchicus*
	Common crane	*Grus sp.*
	Pigeon	*Streptopelia spp.*
	Little owl	*Athene sp.*
	Magpie	*Pica pica*
	Eurasian Tree sparrow	*Passer montanus*

larly revealing to read the list of courses for a festive banquet given in 709 in honor of a gentleman called Wei Juyuan, to mark his appointment to high public office. The *Shipu* lists the fifty-eight dishes, and although we cannot reconstruct recipes from the brief descriptions, they give an idea of the rich assortment of ingredients, which included deer, bear, donkey, raccoon dog, goose, duck, turtle, and frogs. According to chapter 6 of the *Wulin jiushi*, written in 1270, dinners consisting of more than 200 different dishes were sometimes served in the Song period.

The ten-course menu served to Emperor Qianlong in 1754 seems fairly frugal by comparison. Not every potentate was so restrained. In the revolutionary year 1911, for example, the dinners served twice daily to Emperor Xuantong consisted of "around thirty dishes," mostly meat, fowl, and vegetables,

> The rich snobs from [the capital] Chang'an have very spicy meat dishes served up to them. But they don't understand anything about the art of drinking, only about getting their glasses filled by [the courtesans in their] red skirts. Slaves to the pleasure of the moment, they seem like a swarm of gnats.
>
> *Zui zeng Zhang mishu* (806)

with hardly any fish and seafood. Yet the delicacies from the court's main kitchens were merely window-dressing, because the emperor barely touched them. He preferred the mouthwatering treats from the kitchen of the imperial family's noblest ladies. At least, this is the story the "last Emperor" told in his autobiography (*Wode qianban sheng*), which he published in 1964 under the name Puyi. The monarch had already been stripped of his powers as a child, and perhaps his memory was rather hazy, not just due to the long time lapse, but also because his memoirs were largely compiled at the "suggestion" of Mao Zedong. This probably means the former emperor was coerced into writing certain passages incriminating or excusing himself.

Excerpt from imperial dinner menu, 1911

Chicken strips with vegetables
Boiled ham
Lamb with spinach and bean curd
Beef strips with vegetables
Sea urchin in duck broth
Glazed duck
Diced pork with broccoli
Fried eggplant
Marinated tripe
Bean curd with bamboo shoots
Venison
Selected vegetables
Bouillon

Wode qianban sheng (1964), pp. 50–51.

The good life was celebrated not only at court and in public officials' residences: Even merchants, who were much lower down in the traditional pecking order, did not have to go hungry. A Japanese official reported in chapter 1 of *Shinzoku kibun*, an account published in 1799, that traders from China who had temporarily settled in Nagasaki led fairly modest daily lives, but entertained their guests lavishly with delicacies such as bear's paws, shark fins, and swallow's nests. Western traders who settled in the coastal cities in the nineteenth century were similarly indulgent. Shanghai was particularly known as a place where people regularly wallowed in luxury, eating splendid dinners that ran to several courses, and drinking sherry, wine, beer, champagne, and port wine.

Even now in China there are tourists or employees of overseas firms who try to evoke the lavish tradition of the colonial rulers. This usually fails to impress, however, because nowadays boozing and boasting have little impact on the Chinese, who have really gained confidence over the past several decades. Anyway, snobs from abroad face stiff homegrown competition. The Chinese have stopped being shy about ostentatiously showing off their wealth through food. The luxury restaurants in the big cities definitely match up to international standards, not just for quality but often in price as well.

Spring banquet (painting, unknown artist, twelfth century)

Meanwhile, at the other end of the social scale, especially among mi-
grant workers laid off in the recent recession, millions upon millions of
people have fallen below the poverty level again and constantly face the
threat of hunger. Moreover, they have no perspective. As their status is
often illegal, they slip through the government social net, which is fairly
wide-meshed anyway, and they often do not even have enough savings
for the journey back home, so they lack the protection their family could
provide. Ultimately, the environment of the megacities offers very little
opportunity for people to sustain themselves without an income.

It was probably easier in the days before the cities were heavily built
up. This is vividly shown by a book originally published in the fourteenth century, the *Jiuhuang benzao*, compiled by Zhu Su, a member
of the imperial household. Famed for its illustrations, it lists the names
of 414 contemporary plants growing in the environs of Kaifeng that
destitute people could eat. Two hundred forty-five species are classified as herbs; eighty, as trees; twenty, as grains; twenty-three, as fruits;
and forty-six, as vegetables. The botanical description for each plant

is accompanied by precise information as to which parts—leaf, fruit, seeds, stem, bark, root, tuber, or sprouts—are edible.

This doesn't mean that in times of crisis people simply had to stroll through the fields and woods to secure their survival. In fact, many of the plants listed in the *Jiuhuang benzao* have relatively little nutritional value, and people would have had to eat large quantities to benefit from them. Moreover, it was not always advisable to live literally from hand to mouth. To give just one example, the roots of the Asian poke (*Phytolacca acinosa*) are only safe to eat after release of their inherent toxins, and this is a relatively complex process. Broadly speaking, some passages in the *Jiuhuang benzao* are reminiscent of pillaging a flowerbed, whereas others read like a pharmacy inventory.

One thing is clear: Many people lived in a state of permanent crisis. John Barrow, who stayed in the country from 1793 to 1794 as a member of a British mission, noted, "in the choice of foodstuffs in China, the difference between rich and poor is greater than in any other country in the world." The revolution of 1911 failed to put an end to this situation. In the ensuing twenty years, workers in Beijing spent 80 percent of their food budget on grains, but only 3 percent on meat and 1 percent on fruit. However, when famine broke out, as in 1920, all that was left to fill the belly was sawdust, peanut shells, and leaves. As we know, even worse was to come at the beginning of the 1960s.

Eating the Class Enemy

It is a well-known fact that extreme situations can cause people to eat human flesh. In China, a country repeatedly afflicted by natural disasters, there are innumerable accounts of desperate acts of cannibalism, often with children as the victims. Sieges of cities created similar states of exigency. Anthropophagy as socially institutionalized behavior occurred much less often, however. Unlike many legends from other parts of the world, Chinese sources often involve individuals claiming they practiced cannibalism on their own initiative.

This is not just a case of the usual stereotyped pictures of strangers or psycho-

The curly-bearded stranger opened his leather case and took out a blood-soaked human head, heart and liver. Tossing the head back into the bag, he cut the heart and liver into strips and ate them with his beer. "That was a man who acted disloyally towards the state," he proclaimed callously.

Qiuranke zhuan (around 900)

paths. On the contrary, the literature is full of admiration for the spirit and daring of anyone who succeeds in completely eliminating an enemy or a rival by ritually eating him. Cannibalism is even associated with the founders of dynasties. Gaozu, the first emperor of the Han dynasty, who reigned from 206 to 195 B.C., is reputed to have personally ordered the eating of human flesh. According to legend, he had the corpse of his enemy, the king of Liang, cut up and cured, and then distributed the "morsels" to his vassals.

If we are to believe the sources, human flesh was baked, roasted, braised, boiled, steamed, stewed, smoked, cured, sun-dried, and pickled. Many accounts, however, were largely metaphorical and rhetorical, and were intended to humiliate the victim. It is impossible to know how far this really aroused fear and horror, but we can well imagine it would have had an intimidating effect in a society that placed high value on being physically intact.

In contrast, there is a series of writings praising the special merit of people who donated their own body parts to help heal family members above them in the hierarchy, specifically parents and in-laws. For instance, a passage in chapter 13 of the *Huaian fuzhi*, a chronicle compiled in 1573, refers to a virtuous woman who was married at the age of fourteen. When her parents-in-law subsequently became ill, she prayed for their rapid healing and cut three pieces of flesh from her own thigh to make a soup. Her in-laws recovered quickly after eating it.

In each case, the donor's gender seems to be directly related to the sources of the story. Whereas male donors dominated in official history writing, women made up the majority in the more informal accounts. The pious members of the younger generation, and sometimes the devoted wife, nearly always ended up surviving, since the operation seldom proved fatal. This is surprising, considering that even vital organs like the liver were used for making remedies, and surgery was generally said to have been performed by lay persons. With this kind of inconsistency, we can assume that many of the stories were purely rhetorical. Nonetheless, there are still genuine cases of self-mutilation today, if only because people don't always realize that the accounts are fictitious, and not meant as practical guides.

A Taiwanese schoolgirl has fed a piece of her own flesh to her mother with terminal cancer in an attempt to cure her. Miss Yang Feng-Huan, a college student, cut the flesh from her arm, and cooked it with Chinese medicine, but the remedy did not work.

South China Morning Post, January 27, 1978

> Hate was officially prescribed, and exter-
> mination quotas were fixed; old cases of
> blood feuds were settled immediately.
> Knives flashed, pieces of flesh flew
> through the air and the gates of hell
> opened wide. When the corpses of the
> "class enemy" were released for con-
> sumption, the political elite opted for the
> heart and liver, while the masses kept to
> arms and soles of the feet.
>
> Terrill (1996)

Anthropophagy has been described as the "most macabre low point of the Chinese cultural revolution." This verdict is largely based on research publicized in 1996 by the author Zheng Yi, who lives in the United States. According to this, between 1966 and 1970 in Guangxi (an "autonomous region" in southern China), thousands of "class enemies" fell victim to cannibalism. There is no doubt that countless atrocities occurred in that period aimed not just at personally denigrating opponents, but even at physically exterminating them. On principle we cannot dismiss the allegation that there were "bubbling pots containing human flesh in front of local government offices." Such excesses were probably the result of taking blustering too seriously, and bore no relation to any authentic tradition.

Young Kitan man dancing (wall painting, 1111)

It would be completely mistaken to link the riots to an alleged custom of the Zhuang, the dominant ethnic minority in Guangxi, as some commentators have suggested. In fact, if the Zhuang were familiar with anthropophagy at all, they saw it as stereotypical behavior of strangers. The alternative explanations are hardly any more convincing. One fantastically concocted, stupid version claims to have discovered the origins of "cruelty and cannibalism" in a "combination of Zhuang culture, Han culture, totalitarian politics, the class analysis of Marxism-Leninism, and the personality of Mao."

Worse than Death: The Diet of Minorities

According to the most recent census (of 2010), around 8.5 percent of the Chinese population belong to an ethnic minority. This may not seem particularly impressive until we remember that the total population is around 1.34 billion, which means minorities account for around 113 million people. Eighteen of the groups listed in the census comprise more than a million people. If we compare this number with the populations of European countries, the demographics of the Zhuang would

> I am Chinese, and our food, drink and clothing are completely different from that found here [in the northern border regions]. [Having to] live like this is worse than death.
>
> Zhang Li, cited in *Jiu Wudaishi* (974), chapter 98

correspond to that of The Netherlands; the Manchurians, to that of Greece; the Hui, to that of Hungary; the Miao, to that of Sweden; and the Tujia, Uyghurs, and Yi, to approximately that of Austria.

Fifty-five "national minorities" are presently recognized in China, some of which—but not all—have a long history. Official recognition was largely determined in the 1950s through a selection process involving a much greater number of claims. Minority status was awarded on the following criteria, borrowed from Stalin: (1) own language; (2) territorial integrity; (3) single economy; (4) sense of common identity.

See Appendix, Table 9.

None of these factors can serve as a universal criterion for determining ethnic membership. The attitude to language, which would seem to be the simplest of the criteria mentioned earlier, illustrates the arbitrary way the bureaucracy works. The officially recognized "nationalities" include, first, groups such as the Manchu, whose members hardly understand their presumed mother tongue any longer, as they mostly speak Chinese now. On the other hand, some groups never had a common language: Sometimes this was because religion was the identifying factor for their members (such as the Muslim Hui); in some cases, such as the Yao, several languages exist within a putative community. Similar reservations apply to the concept of "territorial integrity." Particularly in northern and northwestern China, the traditional pastoral economy demands a high degree of mobility.

The Chinese authorities have always been deeply suspicious of a way of life not based on settlement. This attitude still pervades today, just as it did more than 2,000 years ago, when the *Shiji* (chapter 110) criticized the "lack of cities and fixed abode." The alleged potential for aggression associated with these groups also affected the treatment of regions

> I was married out
> to the place where the sky ends. . . .
> Now I sleep in a felt-covered tent
> and feed on raw meat
> and mare's milk.
> My heart is heavy—
> how I long to return!
> If I were a yellow crane
> I could fly home this very day.
>
> Xijun, cited in *Hanshu* (115), chapter 96

inhabited by autochthonous groups. Whereas the south was seen as quite "natural" territory for expansion, there was a generally defensive attitude toward the north. Still, over the centuries a number of steppe peoples managed to expand their kingdoms into the Chinese heartland. The most successful were the confederations of the Tuoba (Northern Wei dynasty, 386–534), Kitan (Liao dynasty, 916–1125), Tanguts (Western Xia dynasty, 1032–1227), and Jurchen (Jin dynasty, 1115–1235). In the end it was left to the Mongols (Yuan dynasty, 1279–1368) and Manchu (Qing dynasty, 1644–1911) to bring the entire empire under their dominion. The list might have gone back in time even further if the Xiongnu had concentrated more on territorial gains than on appropriating possessions, for the Han court succeeded in restraining their attacks simply with splendid gifts and clever marriage politics. It was the princesses who suffered, for they were given away to "barbarian nobles." Among them was Xijun, a poet and granddaughter of Emperor Wu, who lived on the threshold of the first century B.C., and complained bitterly about the dietary habits in the steppes.

Today's minorities in China's northern border regions still live on a diet based largely on meat and milk products. When the Mongols gather for a celebration they serve their traditional festive stew, *horhog*. The main ingredient is a freshly slaughtered lamb that is cut into large pieces

---

LAMB SKEWERS (XINJIANG: UYGHUR)

Ingredients

2 lb (1 kg) lamb (not too lean)
4 tbsp cumin
2 tbsp ground chili pepper
2 tbsp salt
Sunflower oil

Preparation method

1. Cut the meat into long, medium thick pieces, and arrange on skewers.
2. Combine the cumin, ground chili pepper, and salt.
3. Cook the skewers on a charcoal grill.
4. Turn several times, sprinkling generously with the seasoning mix.
5. Drizzle with oil if required.

Note: Best served with flatbread.

and cooked using stones heated on an open fire, then arranged in alternating layers with the bones in a container. In the past a sheepskin was used as the cooking vessel; today it is likely to be a large pot normally used for carrying milk. Vegetables such as potatoes, carrots, turnips, and onions can be added, and it is seasoned with garlic, local herbs, pepper, and salt, but in relatively small quantities to preserve the strong flavor of the lamb. The gentle cooking effect is achieved by adding water to create steam, and therefore pressure, before closing the "pot."

Cheese is another staple food, because it keeps well, but it is sometimes dried for so long on the yurt roof that it is too hard to bite and almost has to be sucked. Westerners may find the taste rather dull. They are far more likely to appreciate the yoghurt, which is usually made from milk of yaks, mares, goats, sheep, and camels, and sometimes served with fruits and sugar.

The minorities living in China's southern periphery also eat dried cheese, but not as a staple food. Fruit and vegetables are more important

---

RICE COOKED IN BAMBOO CANE (TAIWAN: TSOU)

Ingredients

4 cups glutinous rice
3–5 finely chopped dried mushrooms
2 tsp Sichuan pepper
1 bamboo cane
Bamboo leaves

Preparation method

1. Wash the glutinous rice and soak in cold water for 3 to 4 hours.
2. Add the mushrooms and Sichuan pepper.
3. Stuff the mixture into a bamboo cane until it is around two thirds full.
4. Add water (but don't fill the cane completely), and seal with the bamboo leaves.
5. Rotate the cane gently, with the opening slanted upward, at the edge of the open fire.
6. Remove from the heat source when the contents start boiling, and continue cooking slowly until the rice is done.
7. Leave the bamboo cane to cool, then cut off the singed part with a knife.
8. Cut the bamboo cane into pieces, carefully remove the contents, and cut into slices.

Note: Aside from mushrooms, other ingredients such as cured meat, shrimps, or fish, can also be added.

in their diet, and in the heavily forested regions of Yunnan mushroom gathering brings variety to the menu in early autumn. While hunting makes a substantial contribution to the diet, meat is generally less important here. The restraints on meat eating are not just due to scarcity, rational arguments, or culinary preferences—they also relate back to mythology. For instance, the Yao, who claim descent from a "dog ancestor," have a strict prohibition on eating canids. Animal products are often cured or cooked at low heat; plant products are frequently dried and pickled; and rice is often prepared by cooking in fresh bamboo stalks.

The same cooking method for rice is also popular among the indigenous population of Taiwan, whom the guidebooks and statistics of the mainland usually refer to as "Gaoshan" or Gaoshanzu (mountain folk), whereas corresponding Taiwanese sources call them Yuanzhumin (autochthonous population). Today they consist of thirteen groups, including the Ami, Atayal, Bunun, Paiwan, Puyuma, Rukai, and Tsou.

The sticky rice is moistened and put into a [still green] bamboo cane. This is laid in the charcoal residue from a fire, and after a short time it is ready for eating.

Zhulo xianzhi (1716), chapter 8

This classification is another product of recent history: It derives from elaborate surveys conducted by Japanese linguists and anthropologists at the turn of the nineteenth century and into the twentieth. Until then, most of the autochthonous population apparently had no sense of common identity beyond their own settlement unit. As a result, most ethnonyms do not have a very long tradition. Often, for each group, the specific common term for "human being" (and the one that is actually somatically understood) is used as the basis for broad linguistic classification, and then transposed onto the resultant "tribes" as a definition.

Chapter Five

Heavenly Dew

Water: Liquid of Life

In China, as elsewhere, water was probably the most important element of nutrition for many centuries, at least for most of the population. According to chapter 91 of the *Hanshu*, a dynastic history compiled at the beginning of the second century, people at the bottom end of the social scale had nothing but "soybeans to chew on and water to drink." At the same time, in ancient compendia of rituals, clear water headed the list of beverages served to members of the ruling family.

The quality of water for refreshment was very important. It is noteworthy that even in the period before the unification of the empire, the most delicious water was thought to originate from remote mountains close to landscapes with mythical associations. Considering the transportation opportunities at the time, it was hardly possible to reconcile the literary yearning for exclusiveness with the real-life desire for freshness. Leaving aside regional categories, however, the main distinctions were clear: whether the water came from a well, from a spring, or from gathering dew.

> One can surely be merry even when eating simply, drinking water, and using the crook of one's arm as a cushion.
>
> *Lunyu* (around 450 B.C.), chapter 7

Wells can quite easily be reconstructed archeologically. Sometimes the walls were simply smoothed down, but particularly in cities they often had an extra lining with well casings made of clay, stone, wood, or woven wattle. Excavations have generally yielded little precise information on the parts of the well above ground, but clay

會昌四年十月冬至後三日和景曼溫於後園高亭披閱太尉平章事

After-dinner nap (scroll painting attributed to Lu Yao, ninth century)

miniatures deposited in tombs are useful for deducing various kinds of rope winches, curbing, and roofing.

Alternative methods were needed to ensure a constant water supply in the deserts at the northwestern boundary of the Chinese kingdom. Even today, the inhabitants there use a system that has worked efficiently in large parts of western and central Asia since ancient times. Known by two names, the Persian, *kariz*, and the Arabic, *qanat*, it consists of underground channels that use height difference to carry the water from the foot of the mountains to the oases without excess loss from evaporation and seepage.

> Hoar frost . . . is swept into a bottle using a hen's feather. If it is tightly closed and stored in a dark place, [the contents] keep for a long time without decaying.
>
> *Yinshi xuzhi* (1350), chapter 1

The exact time of use was also important, particularly for dietetics, and collected rainwater was only considered usable if it did not come from a heavy storm. At least, this was noted by the *Yinshi xuzhi*, compiled in 1350, which distinguished between more than two dozen different types of water with respect to their healing effects. The list ranges from thermal springs to liquefied ice. Here too people generally regarded a remote place of origin as proof of superior quality.

Mineral sources were apparently used from early on, but it seems that carbon dioxide was only added at the instigation of the West. In fact, soda, which was commercially available in the big cities from around the mid-nineteenth century, was initially called *helanshui* ("Dutch water") in Chinese. Before long, artificial flavoring and coloring were added, and a wide range of fizzy drinks appeared on the market. Yet consumption of soft drinks is still modest despite the enormous growth in recent years, largely through demand from the young urban population. As regards mineral and table water, annual consumption per head in liters has stayed relatively stable, and has not risen above single figures.

Sipping iced drinks for refreshment in the hot season of the year used to be a privilege reserved for the upper classes. Particularly on a journey, however, even "ordinary" people made a point of carrying boiled water with them. The first recorded mention of this hygienic practice appears in chapter 1 of the *Jilei bian*, a source from the twelfth century. It is rather surprising that it entered the literature so late, but this is probably because it was seen as an obvious precaution, and not worth mentioning. Nowadays hot *kaishui* is widely available from drink dispensers or Thermos flasks and is preferable to drinking water directly from the tap.

> When you open [the mineral water bottle] the stopper flies towards you. You should watch out that it doesn't hit your eyes or [other] parts of your face. If you drink the water directly it cools you down immensely.
>
> *Huyou zaji* (1876), p. 40

Whatever the occasion, you should be careful when quenching your thirst, because what you may think is refreshing can easily end up in retching—or something worse, if the drink is contaminated with any kind of toxic substance. The barrels and tubs from which traveling tradesmen sold water in China until well into the twentieth century have been replaced almost everywhere by a rather haphazard supply network, but built-in filtration machines frequently work badly if the original source is not adequately protected against pollution. Although chlorine is often added (sometimes excessively) to combat contamination, this is not a universal practice.

Teatime in Paradise

The best way to picture the everyday life of the upper class in the eleventh century is to look at the graves built in northeastern China under the rule of the foreign dynasty Liao. A good example is the wall paintings in a family burial ground in Xiabali (Hebei province), which show several tea preparation scenes. The picture on the east wall of the antechamber of Tomb 7 is particularly charming. The tomb contains the ashes of Zhang Wenzao, who was buried in 1093, although he died nineteen years earlier. The picture shows eight people, including some happy children, grouped around a dresser and two tables. Several objects required for preparing tea can be identified on the floor: a tea grinder, and a lacquer tray containing a knife, a bamboo brush to whisk the liquid, and a tea cake, together with a teapot on a charcoal stove.

The grinder is similar to a silver object that was discovered among the treasures in excavations of the Famen monastery (Shaanxi province) in 1987. It has been identified as a gift donated by Emperor Xizong in 874. Beside it, archaeologists found a little sieve pan, two baskets, and other boxes and spoons, also of silver, as well as several small bowls made of glass and fine ceramic ware: in other words, a wide variety of objects that can be associated with preparation and enjoyment of tea.

Making tea (wall painting, 1093)

The accessories described in the extensive tea literature are even more ingenious. For example, the *Chajing*, written by Lu Yu in 760 as the first compendium of its kind, already refers to no fewer than twenty-four accessories, including—alongside the objects mentioned earlier—various strainers, brushes and tongs, a measuring beaker, a water container, a jug, and a cleaning cloth. By contrast, the *Chaju tuzan*, written in 1269 and notable for its well-illustrated instructions, made do with exactly half of the appliances. Even the court could sometimes be modest: the *Daguan chalun*, written by Emperor Huizong in 1107, listed just five utensils.

Many treatises on tea are notable for a kind of purism in specifying the individual steps in tea making and rejecting any additives, but this type of pedantry had only limited success. Large

> Although tea has its own flavor, in the case of goods destined for the court, ambergris or fat are often added to intensify the taste. . . . Fruits and herbs are also used for that purpose, but with even worse results. We strongly recommend avoiding such additives.
>
> *Chalu* (1051), chapter 1

sections of the population lacked the equipment and time to follow the complicated directions we can easily imagine from looking at the modern Japanese tea ceremony. Mostly they preferred infusions that included parts or preparations of substances such as ginger, scallions, jujube, orange, Japanese dogwood, peppermint, cloves, camphor, and musk mallow. Salt was obviously one of the most important ingredients. Today it is considered trendy to follow Western habits by adding milk and sugar. Most of the other flavorings come from blossoms, especially jasmine, chrysanthemum, and rose.

Since ancient times, the basic ingredients of Chinese tea have been the leaves of the tea bush, which was already cultivated in southwestern China before the unification of the empire, primarily in the area of today's Sichuan province. Under the Han dynasty it gradually spread to the central and eastern regions of the country. Compared with the *assamica* variety grown mainly in India, the Chinese plant's yields are not particularly high, but it compensates by being sturdier and less sensitive to cold and arid conditions.

Tea is normally classified on a scale from untreated "green tea"—with some intermediary stages—to fully fermented "red tea," which is called black tea in the West. If the product is destined for a superior category, the exact growing area and harvest date are also important. Of course, only connoisseurs are able to guess from the label what awaits their taste buds: the names given to different teas are just as imaginative as

TEA EGGS

Ingredients

6 eggs, 3 tbsp tea

Preparation method

1. Hard-boil the eggs (for around 10 minutes), refresh, and crack the shell by pressing the egg in your hand or rolling it on a firm surface to create fine cracks, but without peeling off the shell.
2. Add the tea leaves to the water from the eggs and bring to the boil.
3. Put the eggs into the pot carefully and leave to simmer for around 30 minutes until the shells change color. Then turn off the heat and leave to infuse until the water gets cold.
4. Peel and quarter the eggs, which are now delicately marbled.

Note: You can enhance the taste by adding spices to the tea in the water such as salt, Sichuan pepper, cloves, star anise, and cinnamon.
Serve as a starter or snack.

any flights of fancy in the culinary vocabulary. Here is just a small selection of examples from different ages: Heavenly Dew, Liquid Jade, Water Nymph, Fragrant Flake, Dragon Well, Lion's Peak, Jewel Cloud, and Heavenly Pillar. Of course, not even the most beautiful name can guarantee the desired refreshment if the tea is brewed without enough attention to quality and the right water temperature.

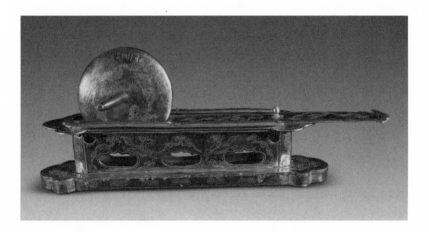

Silver tea grinder (ninth century)

Green tea, a beverage made from a leaf infusion, stands for subtle simplicity and contemplative pleasure in the West as well as in China. However, the apparently simple way of preparing it was probably an exception under the Tang and Song dynasties, as were some of the processing methods later considered typical, including withering, stir-frying, drying, and fermenting. Until the thirteenth century, after harvesting and quality classification treatment of the leaves preferably involved three processing stages: (1) heating in steam, (2) stamping or pressing and rolling, (3) forming into cakes or tiles with a firm consistency. Before hot water could be added, the cake mass had to be pulverized using a grinder or pestle and mortar, and strained several times; sometimes this was preceded by a roasting process.

> The first bowl wets my lips and throat,
> the second dispels melancholy.
> The third bowl steeps my parched
> entrails:
> The place of five thousand volumes I
> have studied.
> The fourth bowl flushes sweat and pain
> from my pores,
> And the fifth purifies my body
> completely.
> The sixth bowl brings me into harmony
> with the immortals,
> But I no longer want to drink the
> seventh:
> caught by the wind that makes wings of
> my sleeves.
>
> *Zoubi xie Meng yongyi xin cha* (835).

Buddhist monks played a key role in the spread of tea drinking, especially the disciples of schools where meditation was important and a quick brew helped to keep them awake. In fact, the stimulating effect of the caffeine develops in the first few minutes after the water is poured onto the tea leaves, whereas the soothing effect of the tannin takes longer to work. It was probably Buddhist dignitaries who made this invigorating drink fashionable, along with their religion, and who were responsible for the Daoist and Confucianist elite developing a taste for tea as well.

It was some time before the mass of the population was able to afford the blissful pleasures of tea drinking, but Heavenly Dew and Liquid Jade were more widely affordable, at least by the time of the Song dynasty, as shown by the numerous teahouses that opened in the cities. They are currently undergoing a revival, although this owes more to well-off tourists than to the local populace. Aside from the high prices, the significant rise

Making tea (wall painting, 1117)

in cultivation and consumption of tea in recent years means tea drinking has lost its special social function. China is now the biggest producer in the world market, with annual production totaling 1.5 million metric tons. Of this, around 310,000 metric tons are exported, more than the total annual yield thirty years ago. The increase is due not only to expansion of tea farming areas, but also to excessive use of chemical pest control. Many analyses of tea grown in China reveal large pesticide residues—and, ironically enough, green tea, which is so often extolled as beneficial to health, has also been found to have high pesticide residues.

An Acquired Taste: Alcohol

Although China has a wealth of terms for alcoholic beverages dating back more than 2,000 years, the history of the drinks is not very easy to trace. Complications arise because the term most often used in the literature, *jiu*, makes no distinction between beer brewed from grain containing starch, wine pressed from fruit containing sugar, and spirits obtained from distilling. The fact that consumers in the West have adopted a vocabulary that also ignores these differences, as in the case of "rice wine," only adds to the confusion.

The word used for beer today, *pijiu*, only dates back to the end of the nineteenth century, following a decision to prefix the general term *jiu* with the character *pi*, which was supposed to sound like Western words such as *beer*. However, the first two elements of the term *putaojiu* (*wine*) date back to ancient Persian. Although the name has very deep etymological roots, the wine tradition in China has a much shorter history.

In prehistoric times, beer was mostly made of millet and rice. By the time of the Shang dynasty, brewing technology was already at a high level, as illustrated by the discovery of a small "brewery" near Gaocheng in Hebei province. Altogether, archeologists found sixty-four containers and tools, some of which still contained traces of ingredients, including yeast; stones from peaches, plums, and jujubes; and hemp and jasmine seeds. The frequent assumption that fruit wine was pressed here is mistaken, however, because the key element was probably foxtail millet, which was found in a storage pit not far away, whereas the other ingredients were merely used for fermenting and improving flavor. The honey found at another location had a similar function; however, adding it to beer does not create mead.

DRUNKEN CHICKEN (TAIWAN)

Ingredients

10 oz (300 g) boned chicken breast
¼ tsp salt
¼ tsp white pepper
1 cup (¼ L) rice wine
1 cup (¼ L) chicken stock
1 tbsp finely chopped ginger

Preparation method

1. Season the chicken breast with salt and pepper, then steam.
2. After cooling, immerse in a mixture of rice wine, chicken stock, and ginger.
3. Refrigerate overnight in a tightly closed container.
4. Cut the chicken breast into pieces and serve cold as a starter or snack.

Several years ago there was great excitement about the news that the earliest site ever discovered for production of wine from grapes had been found in China. In fact, although traces of wild vine had been found on pottery dating back to the seventh millennium B.C. in Jiahu (Henan province), analyses also revealed remains of rice, honey, and other fruits. In this case, as in many others, we can infer that the cereals were the dominant components and the other substances (such as vine traces) were simply additives. This is also well documented for later periods: For example, there is a description in chapter 3 of the *Beishan jiujing*, written at the beginning of the eleventh century, of how "ground apricot kernels and grapes" were mixed into the rice during the fermentation process.

Unlike sugary fruits infested with yeast fungus that start fermenting without human intervention, grains need added enzymes to create maltose from the starch; the maltose then separates into alcohol and carbon dioxide. Since ancient times, highly elaborate recipes have been used to produce the ferment (*qu*), and the brewing process sometimes took several weeks or months. Cereals, usually wheat, rice, or millet, were always the main ingredient, and there were an enormous number of additives. Ginseng, ginger, and nutmeg were especially popular.

To achieve the desired taste, spices such as cardamom, cloves, and cinnamon were also added at later stages of brewing. In the Song period lamb stock was used, and the resulting Lamb Beer was famous throughout China. Aside from the odd combination of flavors, this hardly satisfies the requirements of the famous German purity law for beer. The producers of the renowned Tsingtao beer (currently exported to sixty-two countries) claim they adhere to German brewing standards. However, the predecessor of this U.S.–Chinese–Japanese consortium, the Germania Brewery established by the German colonial masters in Qingdao in 1903, already cheated at some point by adding rice to the prescribed water, hops, and malt.

> Yeasts are produced from a wide variety of substances and additives, while there are innumerable varieties . . . of the] flavoring herbs that go into winemaking. They range from a few to some hundred ingredients. . . . Smartweed is the spirit of the yeast, and grains are the body.
>
> *Tiangong kaiwu* (1637), chapter 17

Other beer producers add sorghum and rye as well. Sometimes, it is said, bitter melon (*Momordica charantia*) is used instead of hops—but in any case, the introduction of European brewing techniques at the end of the nineteenth and the beginning of the twentieth century, initially by German, Russian, and Czech specialists, finally put an end to the indigenous Chinese brewing tradition. The great success story, however, did not begin until the 1980s, when the beer trade, which had merely drifted along under Communist rule, received a fresh injection of Western expertise that led to massive improvements in product quality and quantity.

Most beer producers use formaldehyde to prevent sediment building during storage, and it is handled with less care in China than in many other countries. Names for beer, such as Snowflake, Sea Pearl, and Moonshine, seem to offer total bliss. Still, the choice of names is more restrained than in the Song period, when consumers could savor the refreshment of Jade Froth, and the promise of sips of Long Life and Eternal Life.

Even in those early days, China was probably one of the leading international producers. Today it undoubtedly produces the world's largest volume of beer, more than 12 billion gallons. In recent years, partnerships with Western investors and oenologists have considerably boosted the importance of wine growing in China as well. In 2010, following several good years with growth rates in double figures, the wine yield totaled around 1,100 million liters. Although this is quite respectable by global standards, per capita consumption of wine in China is still relatively low.

Yet viticulture, unlike brewing, has not been widely accepted on a continuous basis. In fact, there was only one period in imperial history when pressed grapes were anything like as important as fermented grain: the time of the Tang dynasty, with its occasional bouts of wild enthusiasm for exotic goods and ideas. Wine played a minor role until then. Probably the earliest recorded mention of wine specifically related to the Middle Kingdom dates from the year 223 during the Wei Dynasty, in an edict from Emperor Wen (reigned 220–226) extolling the merits of the beverage.

> There are a huge number of choice fruits in China. Let's return to the subject of wine grapes. . . . They [exude] a long lasting aroma, are very juicy, dissolve worries, quench your thirst, and can also be fermented to make alcohol that is sweeter than beer. You can get fairly drunk on it, but sober up easily again afterwards. . . . No other fruit can compare with this.
>
> *Zhao qun chen* (223).

Before then the grapevine was indigenous only as a cultivated plant in the parks and gardens of the nobility. Several sources, including *Shiji* and *Hanshu*, associate its introduction with the year 126 B.C., when General Zhang Qian (195–114 B.C.) returned to the capital from a diplomatic mission to Central Asia and brought some rare specimens with him. Domestic wine products were not yet available during the Han period, however; the Chinese had to be content with some rare wines that made the long journey of several thousand kilometers from faraway Western lands. In contrast to other alcoholic beverages that farmers produced (including drinks from pears, jujube, or palm juice), wine from grapes remained a luxury item in the following centuries, and its consumption was restricted to a small, elite group. The basic ingredient was always *Vitis vinifera*; as yet there is no evidence to support the occasional claim that wild vine species could have been used to make wine.

Winegrowing still had close ties to the imperial court at the beginning of the Tang period, and the dynasty's first two emperors Gaozu (reigned 618–626) and Taizong (reigned 627–649) are said to have shown great interest in it. Chapters 4 and 7 of the *Qimin yaoshu*, an agricultural manual written around 540, describe in detail how grapes were treated, from storage to raisin production. Yet this work, which is otherwise very comprehensive, does not mention wine making; nor does the poetry of the following centuries, which speaks of vine cultivation, irrigation, and grape picking but not of the final step towards fermentation as an organized process.

Cultivated tipsiness and the resulting hangover was a common theme of lyrical poetry. Despite Cao Pi's upbeat description, this could certainly have unpleasant and lingering effects, particularly because of rather haphazard dilution and, as with beer, the variety of additives that were mixed in. Moreover, the resulting liquid was generally drunk warm, which gave it the taste and effect of a slightly stale version of the mulled wine we drink today, rather than a quality beverage served at the right temperature.

The most famous grapes of all were called "mare's tits" because of their elongated form, in contrast to the rounded type, known as "grass dragon beads." Other descriptions, such as "crystal," or "purple," refer to the color. The names for grape varieties introduced in the last century are also very picturesque: Dawn Pearl (Cabernet Sauvignon), Sweet Sunset (Saperavi), Nobles' Fragrance (Riesling), and Jade Syrup (Gewurztraminer).

At least by the Tang period, the area around the city of Taiyuan in Shanxi province had become a leading viticulture center. Other long-standing traditional centers are the wine-growing area in the Hexi Corridor in the autonomous region Ningxia in Gansu province, and Turfan in the autonomous region Xinjiang. Yet more important today are the comparatively young vineyards in northeastern China in the provinces of Hebei, Shandong, and Liaoning. Vines are even cultivated south of the twenty-fifth parallel in places such as Yunnan province, where the wine growers produce a very palatable variety at altitudes of almost 2,000 meters.

> The capital of the province . . . is called Tiananfu [Taiyuan]. They produce so much wine there. . . , they can even supply the surrounding provinces.
>
> Marco Polo (around 1300), Book 2, chapter 29 [Fol. 34r]

Nowadays China produces respectable varieties of sparkling wine. It took almost a century, however, to develop indigenous types that could seriously challenge the initial dominance of imports, mainly from France. The Chinese name for sparkling wine, *xiangbin*, can be traced back (via English) to the French word *champagne*, but we should not assume from this that only quality brands were available. Perhaps this explains why champagne has not been universally welcomed, as an early-twentieth-century satire quoted in the box at the bottom left of this page illustrates.

> He sipped cautiously at the brimming champagne glass, frowned and shouted, "This isn't alcohol, it tastes like vinegar. Just look at how the stuff fizzes; it's completely undrinkable."
>
> "It's supposed to be like that," they told him . . . , "it tastes perfectly all right once you get used to it."
>
> Xin shitou ji (1905), chapter 9

Drinking sparkling wine was largely an urban pastime, and few people could afford such ostentatious luxury. Alongside the shady dives where bar girls boosted the takings, the drink was used to add a festive touch to official events from quite early on. No banquet was complete without sparkling wine, and not just for entertaining Western colonial dignitaries in the past, but even at state receptions in the twenty-first century. The Chinese are also fond of toasting the signing of a contract with a glass of Imperial Court or Prosperity.

Liquors are also served at receptions, of course. *Maotai*, for instance, is produced in the town of the same name in Guizhou province. It is renowned in China, is widely available abroad, and plays an important role in diplomatic and business life. Made from sorghum and wheat, its alcohol content after several distillations can reach up to 55 percent. Demand is enormous, and there are often supply shortages despite the high price for Chinese customers.

> Champagne has already become very popular. The Chinese adore this sweet, fizzy drink, and the scholar-officials are aware that the Europeans of the coastal cities would not allow a banquet to be celebrated without sparkling wine. This is the reason why, whenever possible, they will present Europeans with this beverage. Basically [the officials] don't understand anything about it, so it's not surprising that in the interior sparkling wines of dubious quality are being peddled [at extortionate prices] by agents of European and Japanese firms with names unheard of [abroad].
>
> Georg Wegener (1926), pp. 49–50 (cited in Frank Dikötter, *Exotic commodities: modern objects and everyday life in China*. New York: Columbia University Press, 2006, 237–38)

The tradition of distilling liquor can be traced back to the late Imperial period in southwestern China, but not (as sometimes claimed) as far back as the Han era. In fact, the arguments for a long tradition are generally tenuous. Some archeologists interpret illustrations on two relief tiles from Xinlongxiang and Pengxian from the first or second century as depictions of the distillation process, but the argument is hardly convincing. Even if we agree with this hypothesis, there is still no proof that the highly alcoholic liquid was made for drinking and not for medicinal use, for example. In any case, contemporaneous written records offer no further clues.

The isolated reference to *shaojiu* in sources from the Tang period is not really helpful in clarifying this, since the term can be translated not only as "distilled alcohol" but also as "heated alcohol," which fits with the conventions of the time related to drinking warm beer and wine. The first reliable descriptions of the distillation process date back to the Yuan dynasty, when China was part of the Mongolian empire. Because this coincided with a crucial phase in technology transfer along the Silk Road, there is

> [*Yalaji*] is a loan word used for alcohol prepared in several stages. . . . The rising steam is like clouds from which the condensation drips like a fine misty rain. . . . At the tasting my friends were told to drink themselves into a stupor, and I had to watch their faces flushing, their eyes misting over, and the spittle dribbling [from the corners of their mouths].
>
> *Yalaji jiu fu* (1344)

good reason to believe that China adopted the earlier-known distillation methods from West Asia, because the terms *alaji* and *yalaji*, which appeared at that time, derive from the Arabian word *'araq* ("sweat"), which has survived into the present as the Middle Eastern word for anise-flavored liquors, and in the names *arak* and *raki* that are familiar to some Western consumers. One of the sources for the phonetic loan is the *Yinshan zhengyao*, compiled in 1330: Chapter 3 mentions "the dew that is obtained during the vaporization of good alcohol and forms the *alaji*."

The best-known types of clear alcohol, aside from *maotai*, include *gaoliang*, which normally has an alcohol content of more than 60 percent and may smell slightly moldy, and *erguotou*, which is lighter, and drunk mainly by ordinary people in the region around Beijing. At least theoretically, both these types are made exclusively from sorghum, whereas *wuliangye* is based on four additional cereal varieties: rice, glutinous rice, wheat, and corn. In fact, we could call China, rather than Germany, the land of *Doppelkorn* (strong corn liquor). There is also a large selection of herbal liqueurs whose additives and flavor often make them difficult to distinguish from medicine. The more palatable varieties include *zhuyeqing*, whose fragrant taste comes partly from bamboo leaves. Although wines are still made today from a large variety of fruits aside from grapes—notably plums and lychees—fruit liqueurs hardly feature at all.

SINGAPORE SLING

Ingredients

1 oz (30 ml) gin
0.5 oz (15 ml) cherry brandy
0.3 oz (7.5 ml) Cointreau
0.3 oz (7.5 ml) Benedictine
4 oz (120 ml) pineapple juice
0.5 oz (15 ml) lime juice
0.3 oz (10 ml) grenadine
A dash of angostura
1 slice of pineapple
1 cocktail cherry

Preparation method

1. Put all the liquids into a shaker and shake on ice.
2. Strain, and garnish with the pineapple slice and cherry.

Serving drinks (stone engraving, 632)

Finally, it is difficult to categorize the different beverages covered by the term *rice wine*. A whole series of them can simply be described as beer, but some brews, such as *shaoxing*, do not fit as easily into this category because of their high alcohol and sugar content; sometimes they also contain highly unconventional additives. The practice of adulteration goes back many centuries in China, but mixed drinks only reached the country through Western influence. There is, however, a world-famous cocktail invented by a Chinese barkeeper: the Singapore Sling, made for the first time by Ngiam Tong Boon (Yan Chongwen), who came from Hainan, in the Raffles Hotel in 1915.

The inhabitants of the steppe zones of northern China, who traditionally subsist on pastoral farming, drink fermented milk, but this is only important for the region. In particular, the descendants of the "horse people," that is, the Mongolians, Kazakhs, and Kyrgyz (the groups often collectively referred to as "Tartars"

This *cosmos* [*kumis*], which is mare's milk, is made in this wise. . . . When . . . [the Tartars] have got together a great quantity of milk] they pour it into a big skin or bottle, and they set to churning it with a stick prepared for that purpose, and which is as big as a man's head at its lower extremity and hollowed out; and when they have beaten it sharply it begins to boil up like new wine and to sour or ferment, and they continue to churn it until they have extracted the butter. Then they taste it, and when it is mildly pungent, they drink it. . . . it leaves a taste of milk of almonds on the tongue, and it makes the inner man most joyful and also intoxicates weak heads. . . .

William of Rubruk (1256), chapter 6; English translation: http://depts.washington.edu/silkroad/texts/rubruck.html#kumiss

in medieval travelogues), make a drink known by the Turkish name, *ku-mis*, or the Mongolian name, *airag*. This is a slightly sour beverage with an alcohol content of between 1 and 3 percent. Whereas milk mainly came from mares and she-camels in the Middle Ages, cow, sheep, and goat products have become more important recently.

After fermentation of the milk, a second production phase can yield liquor, albeit with a rather low percentage of alcohol. It is no longer possible to determine exactly when production of these spirits first began, but the names for them (from *'araq* to *arkhi*) suggest that distillation here, as in the Chinese heartlands, dates back to the Yuan dynasty. What we do know is that technical knowledge that was formerly passed on within the kinship group is dying out: for example, *vodka* has replaced *milk spirits* as the key term in the vocabulary of alcohol production.

Drunk and Dry

As we have seen, the Franciscan missionary William of Rubruk attributed "drunkenness" solely to "weaklings." This is not just ethical bigotry: He failed to understand that, although fermentation counteracts the lactose intolerance that affects 90 percent of the population of China and its neighboring countries, it only alleviates one problem, because alcohol intolerance is widespread as well. Like other enzyme deficiencies, it is largely genetically determined. It slows down the metabolism and raises acetaldehyde levels, causing a series of problems from facial flushing and nausea to rapid heart rate and liver damage.

> I drink alcohol the whole day, but never more than half a pint [5 ge/67 ml], for among those in the world who tolerate it badly, nobody suffers worse than me. . . . But there is also nobody under the heavens who is more partial to it than me.
>
> *Shu Donggaozi zhuan hou* (1096)

Socially isolated alcoholics as a type exist in China, but they tend to be the exception. Drinking has usually been regarded as a social activity, not just in the ritual context of antiquity but also in the conventions of later periods that were heavily influenced by communal consumption. Through the ages, new social standards were repeatedly set to prevent excesses getting out of hand.

In 1606, Yuan Hongtao wrote a wicked satire on the mania for regulation. Having founded the "Grape Society," seven years earlier with some friends, he now proceeded to draw up a satirical list of directives in his "Boozing Statutes," the *Shangzheng*. The treatise began by asserting that uncontrolled tippling was to be prevented by a two-man directorate that would monitor the proceedings of meetings and the sale of drinks. The articles of association also included ideas about the right occasion, timing, and company for a drinking bout, usually balancing positive and negative factors. One paragraph, for instance, listed "13 pleasant and 16 annoying attendant circumstances" for a get-together. The annoyances included miserly landlords, rude guests, disobedient servants, bad lighting, surly faces, rambling thoughts, exaggerated mockery, and secretive sneaking off. The statutes also covered furnishings, tableware, and food and drink, and there were penalties for derelictions.

Playing drinking games was not freely permitted either. Drinking contests were very popular, particularly in the late imperial age. "Wine clubs," societies that existed around the mid-nineteenth century, were described by the missionary Justus Doolittle, who worked in Fujian from 1849 to 1864; and there were also informal gatherings. Historical records going even further back describe types of drinking contests in which the players might have to fulfill tasks requiring a respectable level of mental proficiency as well. They included reciting impromptu poems based on set quotations or ideographs, sometimes with specific rhyme schemes.

This apparent continuity over the centuries may well be explained by the historical sources' exclusive focus on elite culture. In fact, there were probably also simpler game variations in ancient times, for heavy gambling was already widespread then. Today's drinkers mostly play games like charades, which involve guessing about given mimed terms, or they draw cards, or throw dice. Other familiar games, such as reciting tongue twisters, rearranging phrases to a set pattern, and answering general knowledge questions, can also be used to determine who, if anyone, should take the drinking cup. Another frequently described game involves two people seated facing each other, waving their hands around in quick succession. To Westerners this often looks like tossing coins, but it is more complicated because the goal is to say the correct number

> Every drinker with a high tolerance level tests his strength with the rhinoceros horn cup; every drinker distinguished by bravado tests his strength at the games board; every drinker with inspiration tests his strength in rhetoric; every drinker with literary talent tests his ability in the poetic arts; every drinker endowed with special talent tests his strength to the point of utter exhaustion.
>
> *Shangzheng* (1606), Article 7

Hit the Seven: starting with the leader, the players count in turn: one, two, three, four . . . when they get to a number containing a 7 (such as 7 or 17), or a multiple of 7 (such as 14 or 21), the person whose turn it is has to keep quiet and knock on the table. If the person says the number out loud, he or she has to drink as a penalty.

Pass the Flower: starting with the leader, who is blindfolded, a flower (or some other object) is handed from one player to the next until the leader shouts, "Stop!" The person holding the object at that moment has to drink as a penalty.

Zuixiang riyue (1991), pp. 136-37

of outstretched fingers at the moment your opponent opens his or her hand.

Alcohol consumption is heavy during all the traditional festivals and holidays throughout the year, and for the various rites of passage through life. At weddings the bride and bridegroom take turns sipping at two cups tied together with a red string, to demonstrate that their relationship is indissoluble. In addition, the bridal couple is supposed to toast each guest in turn, which can obviously challenge their alcohol tolerance very quickly, making them drunk on something other than happiness. Incidentally, "draining the drink of happiness" is more than a minor element in the complex process of contracting a marriage. In fact, the drinking is regarded as the symbolic implementation of the whole act, and the term used for it is almost a synonym for wedding celebrations. According to legend (*Liaoshi*, chapter 7), there was once a time when drinking alcohol was directly associated with female fertility. At the Liao court in the tenth and eleventh centuries it was supposed to be common practice during the imperial wedding ceremony for the emperor's bride to offer a jug of beer to a woman who was regarded as particularly fecund, to win a share in her fertility.

The "happiness drink" at the wedding corresponds to the "sadness drink" at the funeral. There are numerous opportunities for serving this. Aside from the fixed feasts in the calendar for general remembrance of the dead, individual ceremonies for dead persons have to be held at specific intervals. The mourning period ends on the third anniversary of the death, when grief is allowed to give way to positive assurance, which means that the remembrance ceremony is often hard to distinguish from a wedding celebration, or from a birth, when alcohol is supposed to be drunk three times in a particular sequence.

Regarding the festivals that structure the year, some treatises contain specific prescriptions for the appropriate emotional mood in each case. People are supposed to drink "merrily" at the spring festival (at the beginning of the new year according to the lunisolar calendar); "decently" at the Dragon Boat Festival (on the fifth day of the fifth month); "lyrically" at the Moon Festival (on the fifteenth day of the eighth month);

and "dreamily" at the Double Ninth Festival (on the ninth day of the ninth month). There is no way of telling how far these rules are obeyed, especially after the fifth glass. Likewise, Article 9 of the *Shangzheng* provides several examples of famous people as a guide to participants in a cultivated drinking bout. The drinking behavior exhibited by the exemplary celebrities ranges from "easygoing" to "civic-minded," from "hasty" to "proud," from "carefree" to "melancholic," and from "eager for self-improvement" to "excited."

Sometimes literature takes a sophisticated intellectual approach to the subject of alcohol. This applies particularly to the poetry of the Tang period, when many poets tackled the theme of enjoying a good drop of alcohol, and its effects—from inspiration to hangovers. The three best-known poets of this era—Li Bo (701–762), Du Fu (712–770), and Bo Juyi (772–846)—each wrote hundreds of poems related to beer or wine.

The writers chose widely differing motifs, introducing psychological elements beyond the rather simplistic categorization in the *Shangzheng*. In this context, forging social bonds could be just as important as describing personal joy and despair. Hymns to conviviality and affirmations of friendship appeared alongside praise of solitude, and countless verses were devoted to alleviating sorrow, the pleasure of forgetting, the fear of awakening, and the quest for inspiration. Finally, there was a spate of reflections on the lot of the poet who believed he could only find the right words when he was well and truly drunk.

The same probably applies to the famous calligrapher and painter, Zhang Xu

> Sitting with a pot of beer among the flowers
> I drank alone, without company.
> Raising my cup, I asked the moon to join me
> With my shadow, that makes us three.
> But the moon didn't feel like drinking
> And my shadow followed me blindly.
> Still, for a moment it was fun with these friends
> gamboling together through the spring.
> When I sang, the moon bobbed along.
> When I danced, my shadow lurched after.
> Slightly tipsy, we got on famously.
> But then came the drunken rush and parted us.
> You see, goodwill can never last.
> Not like the starry sky that always quenches longing.
>
> *Yuexia duzhuo* (744)

> There's [only] one reason why I drink: to write poems
> till I'm completely befuddled.
>
> *Zui zeng Zhang mishu* (806)

> Wang Mo [who died at the beginning of the 9th century] loved alcohol, and whenever he began working on a hanging scroll, he started drinking. After he got tipsy he used to enjoy spraying ink around and smearing it with his hands, laughing and singing all the while. Painting with sweeping brushstrokes, and using lighter and darker shades, he [finally] created structures that turned into mountains, rocks, clouds, and water.
>
> *Tangchao minghua lu* (around 845), chapter 30

The calligrapher Zhang Xu (painting by Liang Changlin, around 1980)

(710–750). A poem about him by Du Fu (*Yinzhong baxian ge*) alleged he only produced "clouds on paper" with his brush after he had drained at least three cups. Like other artists with a penchant for performance, he is supposed to have dipped his hair in ink on occasions to paint with it, which earned him the nickname "crazy Zhang." He is usually mentioned together with a younger artist, Huai Su (737–798), a Buddhist monk whose dynamic writing style was inspired by heavy consumption of beer and wine, and who went down in literature as "drunken Su."

Aside from artists, "professional groups" especially at risk from alcohol abuse included reigning monarchs. At least, this is the impression from historical accounts, which often implied that the last representatives of a dynasty in particular had forfeited their legitimacy to govern because of dissoluteness. This began as early as the fall of the royal houses of Xia and Shang; their heads, Jie and Zhou, were said to have destroyed the state in the second millennium B.C. by setting up "meat forests" and "beer ponds" on the instigation of seductive women.

Moral decay caused by alcohol addiction or sexual flings would ultimately color the image associated with certain emperors later on. This is not necessarily wrong, because many "sons of heaven" indulged in considerable licentiousness. Yet it should be noted that the literary contours of a "wastrel" generally only emerged posthumously, after the rulers of the succeeding dynasty commissioned a "historical" verdict. It was certainly convenient to secure ideological backing by using moral superiority retrospectively to legitimate the assumption of power.

Aside from the debate on political responsibility and ethical standards, abstinence is only rarely preached, and the majority of literary texts extol drunkenness. This particularly applies to the poetry of Tao Yuanming, who criticized the lack of possibilities for agreement between advocates of abstinence and supporters of alcohol in his poem cycle *Yin jiu ershi shou* (No. 13), published in 403. Comparing two men, one who "drinks in solitude" and the other who is "sober all year round," Yuanming said he preferred the first because his relaxed attitude was simply "wittier and more stimulating."

> They refuse the offer of drink, they are entirely dedicated to worldly fame.
>
> *Yin jiu ershi shou* (403) No. 3
>
> It is better to drain one more cup in your lifetime, than [fall victim] after death to the fame of a thousand generations.
>
> *Xing lu nan* (744), No. 3

Chapter Six

Regulations and Conventions

Control and Decay

After the unification of China in 221 B.C., the House of Qin made it a priority to establish unified standards throughout the country, including a legal code, currency reform, modification of the written language, and standardization of weights and measures. Although it profited the emperor to establish compatibility in his rapidly growing territory, the main objective was probably to demonstrate his claim to supreme power.

Archeological finds show that even under the inflexible Qin dynasty the threat of heavy penalties failed to prevent deviations from established standards. For example, weights from the third millennium B.C. that were marked as weighing one *jin* (256 g) varied between 234.6 g and 237.8 g, and there were similar discrepancies for volumes. Although such inaccuracies cannot always be explained, contemporary legal texts show they were often the result of deliberate manipulation to maximize profits for individual civil servants and private persons.

Beyond the political mission, and the fear that taxes in the form of payment in kind might yield too little, Qin Shihuangdi, the First Emperor, who reigned from 221 to 210 B.C., was mainly interested in power, and cared little about the correct calibration

> The emperor issued an edict to standardize measurements . . . that called for deviations to be prohibited and ambiguities eliminated. Despite the directive, . . . people no longer keep to the standards set back then. This reversion is part of the natural course of things, but if [the growing trend] continues, there will be nothing left of all the splendid achievements.
>
> Common inscription on weights and measures (third century B.C.).

of market scales and measuring jugs. However, the state authorities, never sparing with regulations, were keen to supervise transactions at the markets, although their main goal was to control the commodity flow rather than protect consumers. As a rule, securing the food supply took precedence over product quality.

At the markets in the Tang period, weapons and silk fabrics were subjected to quality control, whereas foodstuffs were not. Registration was required only for trading with animals used for riding and working. Pigs, sheep, and poultry could be sold with relatively little red tape. The royal court was the only place where everything was always completely supervised. According to the penal code that came into effect in 653, trespassing in the palace kitchen could result in lifelong banishment. Cook and taster were both extremely high-risk professions, because any divergence from normal standards, including the wrong temperature or unsuitable seasoning, was treated as a crime.

(1) Any breach of the legal regulations for preparing dishes for the emperor will result in strangulation of the person responsible.

(2) If food or drink is contaminated, this will be punished by two years' forced labor.

(3) If [only] the ingredients are contaminated, or foods are served to the emperor out of harmony with the four seasons, the penalty is reduced by two degrees.

(4) If the meals were not tasted beforehand, the sentence is one hundred blows with a heavy stick.

Tanglü shuyi (653), Article 103

In terms of food regulations, little has fundamentally changed for the mass of the population since ancient times. The existing food law has recently been amended several times at short intervals, but some of the regulations are very broad. The regulations for describing the origin and quality of wine seem astonishingly lax: the label on the bottle can claim a specific year of origin even if up to 20 percent of the content is from other harvests. One recent positive sign is an apparent decline in the practice of including information on labels solely for the sake of numerical symbolism (the year 1988 was considered especially lucky).

With around a dozen ministries sharing responsibility for implementing unified standards, there are predictable arguments about jurisdiction. Establishing an independent watchdog administration for food and drugs has scarcely improved the situation. Its founding director, Zheng Xiaoyu, was charged with corruption after only four years in office and was executed in 2007. We can hardly assume this worked as a deterrent.

Serious toxic pollution of foodstuffs still occurs regularly, sometimes as a result of insecticide residues or deliberate use of additives. To cite just a few examples, tests between 2003 and 2009 found lead in noodles, formaldehyde in blood sausage, ferrous sulfate in bean curd, DDT in canned vegetables, methamidophos in filled pasta, dichlorvos in ham, antibiotics in fish, aldicarb in ginger powder, and Sudan dyes in spicy condiments. Aside from chemical additives, sometimes odd cases of imaginative doctoring occur: In 2004 it was revealed that several food producers had used human hair, partly obtained from hospitals, in manufacturing soy sauce.

The gap between public promises and economic aberrations was shown most clearly in relation to the Beijing Olympic Games. The Chinese were far more concerned with polishing their image than improving supervisory mechanisms. A joint declaration signed by 300 well-known food producers in Xi'an in April 2008 had no effect. In the same year, investigations revealed that several firms had tainted milk powder with melamine, an industrial chemical used in making glue and detergents. Since melamine is nitrogen-based, food analysts recorded increased nitrogen content and concluded this meant higher protein content. This effect was used in manufacturing chocolate, cookies, and toffees, for example. In this case, however, it was used for baby foods, with tragic results. A number of infants died, and thousands of others suffered severe kidney damage.

The milk scandal was only exposed after the casualties had become too numerous for the authorities to cover up, and massive public pressure prevented them from playing down the issue. By that time, several months had elapsed and some traces had already been obliterated. This is not an isolated case, for a number of officials receive what could euphemistically be called "income supplements" from the food producers. This obstructs thorough investigation and cushions unpleasant consequences if disclosure becomes unavoidable. Most important, the public is not adequately warned about possible health risks. Even worse, all too often those responsible for the abuses do not have to fear sanctions, in contrast to the whistleblowers who publicly expose the scandals. Ultimately, the one thing China's rulers want is to avoid public unrest.

As a result, the press generally keeps silent until the facts are known anyway and it is impossible to shirk reporting them. Yet there are still some journalists who refuse to be deterred. Although critical voices hardly get any hearing in the state-run media, the Chinese are increasingly turning to the Internet to bring up inconvenient questions. Zhou Qing is probably the best-known author to tackle the topic of food safety in recent years. His disturbing observations, published in 2004 as a book, *Min yi he shi wei tian*, attracted a great deal of attention in the West as well as in China. It became a wake-up call, and earned him a nomination for one of Germany's most prestigious literary awards and a ten-month residence in Cologne as a visiting writer.

> Chinese New Year cakes are always eye-catching, but their pretty exterior often conceals risky ingredients [made of substances] that contravene the law. A store in the Shanghai district of Huangpu [. . .] prolongs the shelf life of its New Year cakes by adding sulfur powder. The white color is achieved by adding industrial bleach, and even cheap sodium hydrosulfite is added to make customers think the cakes are really fresh.
>
> *Zhongguo de shipin anquan konghuang* (2006), part 2, p. 1

Although China has no legal provisions for animal protection so far, activists are becoming increasingly vocal. They have chalked up at least one victory by initiating heated debate about a draft law published in January 2010 that includes clauses making it a penal offense to eat dogs and cats. As yet, however, there is no date for the passage of this bill. Interestingly, the loudest public protest is usually reserved for ill treatment and slaughter of "cuddly animals," rather than the disgraceful circumstances in which pigs, ducks, and chickens are kept: The hygienic conditions at battery farms are rarely discussed.

> It is quite wrong for a civilized person to [mistreat poultry] while they are still alive. The feet of live geese should not be roasted on burning coals, and chicken livers should not just be cut out with a knife. Why not?—because animals are meant for human consumption and it is quite admissible to slaughter them, but not to torture them to death.
>
> *Suiyuan shidan* (1790), chapter 2

Meanwhile the media have good reasons for advising against eating dog meat, which is very popular, especially in the winter months: not to support dog owners who get nauseous looking at the dog collars sometimes left lying on the meat counters, but because consumption has become risky. Although most of the dogs come from specialized breeding farms, a good number are stolen by thieves who grab them in the streets, increasingly using poison bait with toxic residues that can be harmful to human health. Infection by parasites is another risk. In meat inspections, even in the twenty-first century, the percentage of dogs infected by trichinosis ran into double figures, and other zoonotic diseases may have equally unpleasant effects.

Cow (horizontal scroll, around 770)

The Lord of the Hearth

For many centuries there was a widespread idea in China that humans had two kinds of soul: the physical soul, *po*, and the spiritual soul, *hun*. The two souls were thought to separate at the moment of death. While the former stayed with the corpse for a time, the latter ascended again to the airy realms of its origin. From then on the descendants of the deceased had to take care of it, including by providing regular food offerings. The custom still persists today, particularly in rural areas.

> In Lu [in today's Shandong province], sacrifices were made every year at Confucius' grave. [. . .] When Emperor Gaozu [who reigned from 206 to 195 B.C.] traveled through the region, he sacrificed animals [namely, a cow, a sheep and a pig].
>
> *Shengjitu* (1544), sheet 52

The earliest written sources, the oracle bones of the Shang dynasty, already mention regular ritual acts of communion with ancestors. Cattle and sheep were often sacrificed, and this was the beginning of a long tradition of animal sacrifices at court that continued until the late imperial era. Gradually, however, the original idea was obscured. Appealing to time-honored custom often became more important than interpreting it, and by the middle of the first century B.C. the ritual had assumed a life of its own. Confucius is also said to have emphasized the continuity of celebrating the rites rather than examining them closely. In fact, the master would probably have been far from happy if he had known that one day he himself would be the object of elaborate rituals, first on a local level and later throughout the empire.

Cattle, sheep, and pigs were the "classical" offerings for many centuries, but other creatures such as dogs, horses, hens, wild geese, and fish were also sacrificed. Important rites often turned into veritable killing orgies as the butchers wielded their knives over and again, thousands of times. The slaughtered animals could be offered in various ways afterward: whole, gutted, or cut into pieces. Whatever the case, the meat was left in its raw state until the end of the ceremony, and only prepared for human consumption later. Elaborately crafted bronze vessels were used for this, especially in the Shang and Zhou periods. Costly tableware was used for serving, and the hierarchical order was strictly observed.

When the personator rose, the ruler and his three ministers partook of what he had left. When the ruler had risen, the six Great officers partook; the officers partook of what the ruler had left. When the Great officers rose, the eight officers partook—the lower in rank ate what the higher had left. When these officers rose, each one took what was before him and went out, and placed it (in the court) below the hall, when all the inferior attendants entered and removed it—the inferior class ate what the superior had left.

"Jitong" chapter in *Liji* (second century).

Liji. Chinese Text Project, translated by James Legge. "Ji Tong":11

http://ctext.org/liji/ji-tong

The custom of distributing fish to underlings was institutionalized in antiquity. It was supposed to demonstrate dependency and social ascent, but could just as well indicate mistrust or a complete fall from grace. In later epochs, too, participation in ritual sacrifices revealed the power relations at court, where officials and eunuchs constantly jostled for influence. The figures speak for themselves: Under the Ming dynasty a workforce of more than 1,000 carefully chosen butchers and cooks was generally available; their sole responsibility was to ensure the smooth conduct of rituals.

Offerings were made not only by the emperor and his immediate circle, but also by his wife and her subordinate concubines.

The selection of sacrificial meals for every day of the year was precisely fixed. Here are just two examples from the complete list given in chapter 2 of the *Jianzhi bian* for the period around 1370: The offerings on the second day of the eighth month consisted of foxtail millet, proso millet, rice, lotus root, taro, kelp, ginger, shrimp, and sugar. Buckwheat noodles, sugarcane, pig, deer, venison, wild goose, swan, cormorant, stork, quail, partridge, and perch were offered on the ninth day of the eleventh month. The combination of foods was not arbitrary. According to Confucian logic, it was designed to follow the rhythm of the seasons.

> A pork knuckle without toes is boiled in clear water until it is soft. The broth is poured off and replaced by one and a half cups of good beer, a sliver of dried orange peel, and five jujubes. As soon as the ingredients are cooked, the pot is removed [from the heat], onions and pepper are added, and more beer is poured in, while the orange peel and jujubes are removed.
>
> *Suiyuan shidan* (1790), chapter 5

The requirement for meals to fit the seasons applied both to the religious sphere and to the everyday life of the elite. Rather than product freshness, it involved implementing a fixed pattern based on the five elements: wood, fire, earth, metal, and water. This gave rise to a real craze for systematization in the Hang period and resulted in people following the dictates of numbers

> Broadly speaking, to preserve harmony, [meals] should be sour in spring, bitter in summer, spicy in fall, and salty in winter.
>
> *"Neize"* chapter in the *Liji* (second century).

RED-COOKED PORK KNUCKLE (CANTON)

Ingredients

1 pig's knuckle from hind leg, the whole rind scored into lozenges with a sharp knife
2 tsp salt
Seasoning mixture made from 8 tbsp soy sauce, 8 tbsp rice wine, and 4 tsp sugar

Preparation method

1. Bring water to the boil in a large pot, add the pork knuckle, and cook at high heat for around 10 minutes; remove and allow to cool.
2. Rub the knuckle with salt and put into a casserole dish with a small amount of water; cover with half the seasoning mixture as evenly as possible.
3. Preheat the oven, then insert the closed casserole dish and cook for around 2 hours at around 150°C; turn several times, basting with the liquid.
4. Dissolve the sugar in the remaining spice blend and pour over the meat. Cook for another 2 hours, turning regularly and basting with the liquid.
5. Remove the meat from the bone and cut into slices. Serve immediately.

TABLE OF SELECTED CORRESPONDENCES WITH THE FIVE ELEMENTS

Wood	Fire	Earth	Metal	Water
East	South	Center	West	North
Spring	Summer	Late summer	Fall	Winter
Sour	Bitter	Sweet	Spicy	Salty
Wheat	Foxtail millet	Sopro millet	Rice	Beans
Liver	Heart	Spleen	Lung	Kidneys

so slavishly that it finally affected even the points of the compass and the seasons.

Cattle were initially indispensable to the "animal sacrifice," but from the ninth century a growing number of Confucians accepted the idea of sparing buffalo and oxen, and rescuing them from the cooking pot. Only "fundamentalists" and certain groups described as "asocial elements" rejected this—and were heavily criticized as a result. In the late nineteenth century they were even compared with totally uncivilized Europeans in Shanghai and Beijing who simply would not go without their steaks. One person who later joined the chorus of critics of tradition was Mao Zedong. Though not generally known for his sensitivity to religious feeling, he denounced slaughter of "invaluable working animals" as early as 1927. This has been forgotten, however, and production of beef has actually increased more than thirtyfold since his death in 1976.

Unlike the Confucians, who opposed asceticism, the majority of Daoists rejected eating meat on principle. Along with prohibiting alcohol, they also objected to eating bulbous plants, radishes, and ginger. They reserved particular disgust for a person who ate the meat of animals from the zodiac cycle that governed his or her year of birth, or that of his or her parents. The zodiac followed a cyclical pattern: rat, cow, tiger, rabbit, dragon, snake, horse, sheep, monkey, cock, dog, or pig. Some Daoist schools exempted deer and pheasant from the prohibition on eating meat, not because wild game had a special status but because those two animals, unlike many others, had no equivalent in heaven.

- You shall not get drunk!
- You shall not eat the meat of six domestic animals: [horse, cattle, sheep, pig, dog, and poultry]!
- You shall not eat the five types of pungent vegetable: [onions, garlic, chives, leeks, and radishes]!
- You shall not kill any living creatures, including insects!

Excerpt from *Taiwei lingshu ziwen xianji zhenji shangjing* (around 370)

MEAT BALLS (JIANGSU)

Ingredients

14.1 oz (400 g) streaky pork, finely minced
3.5 oz (100 g) prawns, deveined and finely chopped
4 dried shiitake mushrooms: soak in warm water, then remove the stalks and cut
   into thin strips
1 chopped onion
4 chopped water chestnuts
1 tsp salt, 1 tsp sugar, a pinch of pepper
2 tbsp soy sauce
1 tbsp cornstarch
8 oz (250 g) spinach or another leafy vegetable
Sauce blend made from ⅛ L stock, 1 tbsp soy sauce, 1 tbsp rice wine, and 1 tsp
   freshly squeezed ginger juice

Preparation method

1. Combine the minced pork, shiitake, onion, water chestnuts, salt, sugar, pepper,
   soy sauce, and cornstarch until they are well mixed, shape into 4 balls, and fry;
   drain off the fat, and keep warm.
2. Blanch the spinach, line the bottom of a fireproof dish with it, arrange the
   meatballs on top, cover, and cook at 170°C for around 20 minutes.
3. Heat the sauce blend and pour over the meatballs. Serve immediately.

Note: In China this dish is known as "Lions' Heads."

Some philosophers regarded the grains harvested on earth as coun-
terparts to the resplendent stars in the sky. It was not only this, however,
that led many Daoist followers to refuse to eat cereals on principle; they
were also genuinely afraid of the risks. They believed cereal consumption could result in malevolent "worms" invading the stomach and
brain, causing pain and gradually draining away life energy. Herbs and
minerals, or water in which the ashes of burned magical charms were
dissolved, were usually recommended as a substitute. Finally, a person's
own saliva and breath were regarded as
alternative forms of food.

Self-denial naturally carried health risks;
even more dangerous was consumption
of substances that were supposed to prolong life, or make people immortal. As
with aphrodisiacs, this mainly involved

The [all-pervading] essence is what
gives life to everything. It makes the five
types of grain appear on the earth below, and the constellation of stars in the
firmament above.

Guanzi (26 B.C.), chapter 2

minerals, including realgar, orpiment, arsenolite, mercury, cinnabar, copper sulfate (vitriol), magnetite, and actinolite. In retrospect, it is hardly surprising that this hastened death rather than delaying it, because even a minor overdose of substances containing arsenic, in particular, could have dangerous consequences. Other substances could also have highly unpleasant side effects.

> Feed a crow . . . with cinnabar and beef until its feathers are completely red. Then kill it, dry [the corpse] in the shade for 100 days and crush it thoroughly in a mortar. If you take the [resulting compound] for 100 days, you can reach a life expectancy of up to 500 years.
>
> *Baopuzi neipian* (around 320), cited from *Taiping yulan* (983), chapter 920

Communal meditation and prayer were much more beneficial. The monks in Daoist monasteries lived quite frugally, and during the Tang era only a light breakfast and one proper meal a day were allowed. The meal was usually eaten in the late morning between 10 A.M. and noon, not to ease hunger pangs but because the top-ranking inhabitants of heaven dined then, and every time meals were synchronized with them it was supposed to prolong a person's lifespan by 400 days. From that meal until the following morning, the monks were only allowed to eat fruit, drink tea and take medication, for demons took nourishment in the afternoons and evenings, and consuming synchronously with them was assumed to shorten one's life by 5,000 days.

The spirits were not the monks' only mealtime companions: There were the other monks and nuns, of course, and the entire procedure, from fetching the tableware to brushing their teeth after eating, was carefully regulated. According to the *Xuanmen shishi weiyi*, which was written at the end of the seventh century, even the pace of eating was subject to strict discipline: "If you are lagging behind, hurry up. . . . If you are ahead of the others, slow down."

> There are Buddhist monks who describe alcohol as "the soup of wisdom," fish as "blossoms floating on water," and chickens as "vegetables growing by the fence." What a waste of time! It only fosters self-deception and makes people jeer.
>
> *Dongbo zhilin* (1101), chapter 2

In some respects Daoists followed Buddhist dietary rules, but they had a different attitude to issues such as stricter meat prohibition. The government authorities, which issued monastery regulations for both religions in the seventh century, encouraged some areas of agreement. The visible differences between the two religions in everyday life were consequently far slighter than the theological differences often aired in fierce polemics. For example, the

Buddhists were particularly fond of joking about the Daoists' restrictions on grains, although only a limited number of Daoists adhered to this.

The discipline that held sway in the monasteries was evidently different from the practice of the outside world, where the majority of lay people did not bother about dietary laws. They generally kept to them only on festivals, when they deliberately ate vegetarian food; otherwise they justified their dietary conduct by scholarly hairsplitting, exploiting the wide scope for interpretation. The many locally based cults were under pressure to find a compromise between dogmatism and tradition, which sometimes led to curious anomalies such as meat sacrifices being offered on Buddha's birthday.

> A person who passed on a cup of beer to drink will be born with only one hand in each of the next 500 reincarnations. How drastic, then, must the consequences be for somebody who actually drank from the cup himself?
>
> *Fayuan zhulin* (668), chapter 93

Although alcohol use was strictly prohibited and only allowed sometimes in special cases for treating serious illness, it played a part in religious rites. That's not the end of the story either. There were actually some confirmed Buddhists who did not regard alcohol as the "root of idleness" but rather as the source of their creativity. Some monks even ran breweries and sold beer. As a rule, however, the "soup of wisdom" was not on the menu at monasteries.

In China, the kitchen god of Western lore was known as the Lord of the Hearth, the God of the Stove, or the Spirit of the Stove. He governed beyond religious and social divides. His worship dated back to the first millennium B.C., and his portrait hung in nearly every household before the Communists took power. The people regularly made offerings to him. They believed this would help them in cooking, and favor other requests they wanted him to grant. Daoists believed he watched over the behavior of individual family members, and passed his observations on to the Jade Emperor, the highest god of the pantheon, which was organized like a temporal bureaucracy. This was supposed to influence the length of a person's lifespan.

This report was issued toward the end of the year. People prayed and offered gifts to the kitchen god for a favorable verdict. Most of the gifts were treats, and the mouth on the image of the god who was supposed to pronounce judgment was often smeared with honey or sugar to induce him to speak "sweet" words, or to glue his lips together to stop him saying anything at all. After the "feeding," the portraits were

MOCK DUCK (SHANGHAI)

Ingredients

10 sheets of dried bean curd skin (*doupi*) from an Asian store, cooked in water
    until soft
8 dried shiitake mushrooms: soak in water for 30 minutes, then remove the stalks
    and slice into thin strips
3 young heads of mustard cabbage, blanched quickly, then finely chopped
60 g canned Chinese preserved cabbage in pickling brine
2 tsp sugar
2 tbsp soy sauce
2 tbsp rice wine
1 cup (¼ L) vegetable stock
A dash of sesame oil

Preparation method

1. Stir-fry the mushrooms, rocket salad, bok choy, rice wine, and half of the sugar
   and soy sauce in a little oil; remove, and keep warm.
2. Brush the bean curd skin with a blend of vegetable stock, sesame oil, and the
   other half of the sugar and soy sauce.
3. Place 5 sheets at a time in layers on top of each other, spread the vegetables
   on top, roll up, and press the edges together firmly.
4. Fry in plenty of oil and cut crosswise into small slices for serving.

Note: Instead of the bean curd skin you can use the dough wrappers normally used for spring
rolls.

removed and burned, to be replaced by new ones after the New Year
festival.

During the Cultural Revolution religious activity was denounced as
counterrevolutionary and could incur draconian penalties. This particularly affected China's Muslims; in some areas they were forced to eat
pork and dog meat against the strict prohibitions of their faith. At that
time, the Lord of the Hearth vanished from kitchens, giving way to portraits of Mao Zedong. The Chairman demanded just as much respect
and ritual attention. In the morning people were supposed to ask him
for instructions, at noon they had to thank him for his magnanimity,
and in the evening they had to report on the events of the day. As if
that were not enough, before every meal they had to chant, "Long live
Chairman Mao and the Communist Party." Despite similarities in worship, there were at least two important differences: First, the party boss

had no superior above him; and second, probably nobody dared to glue up his mouth and burn his image.

Meanwhile, the Lord of the Hearth has ousted the Great Chairman again in many places, although the two of them sometimes hang on the wall side by side in peaceful coexistence. In this way, tradition lives on. At the same time, there are always fresh adaptations, such as the trendy master chef in Hong Kong who made an obvious reference to old customs by dubbing himself the "kitchen devil," and completing the picture with a prominent matching tattoo on his upper arm.

The Right Diet

Dietetics is a big area of experimentation, and a highly promising commercial prospect. In the West it attracts many people trying to escape the complexity of modern life by adopting explanatory models from outside their own culture. Most of these models are legitimated in terms of pseudomythical traditions. Nobody would question the value of a balanced diet, or the importance of a wide range of experience. But what if the underlying system is related not to precise examination of the state of health but to correspondences based on supposedly "magic numbers"?

That is exactly what is involved in subsuming everything under the sequences of the five phases and the duality of yin

> People who know how to compensate for health deficiencies with the help of [adequate] nutrition, how to subdue emotions and alleviate suffering, can rightly claim to master the medical arts.
>
> *Beiji qianjin yaofang* (652), chapter 26

and yang. This classification model was undoubtedly an enormous achievement 2,000 years ago but was heavily criticized even back then because it tried to squeeze every aspect of life into a rather rigid scheme. In the context of cooking, this means (to mention just some of the most important aspects) categorizing individual foods according to their flavor (sour, bitter, sweet, spicy, or salty), their relation to their functional circle (liver, heart, spleen, lungs, or kidneys), their temperature (from cold to hot), and their locus of action (superficial or deep). A sixth, "neutral" category was added later, and

> A person who gets ill and is harmed through treatment by a quack [. . .] should rather have learned a few timely facts about how to deal with his body, and taken care of it before any [health] problems appeared.
>
> *Yu jian zashu* (eleventh century)

> **NUTRITIONAL ERRORS DURING PREGNANCY AND THEIR EFFECTS ON THE BIRTH AND HEALTH OF THE CHILD**
>
> Donkey meat — contagion
> Mule meat — high-risk delivery
> Mulberries and duck's eggs — breech birth
> Frozen spice paste — miscarriage
> Goat's meat — strong predisposition to illness
> Rabbit meat — muteness, harelip
> Chicken and glutinous rice — tapeworm
> Hen's egg and dried fish — frequent abscesses
> Turtle meat — short-necked
> Sparrow's meat and bean paste — dark facial pigmentation
> Sparrow's meat and alcohol — sensuality
>
> *Yinshan zhengyao* (1330), chapter 1.

Buddhist healing arts and Western medicine have also left their traces. The correspondences are often supplemented by analogies, but they tend to be rather simplistic.

There are two distinct basic approaches in Chinese dietetics: the preventive approach, which concentrates primarily on guarding against sickness; and the curative approach, where the goal is to heal an already diagnosed illness. Perhaps we should also distinguish between the rather vague application of dietary rules in restaurants and types of therapy that rely on an individual anamnesis focused on many different factors.

However, the dividing lines are not always clear, and some household remedies actually have their roots in nutritional science.

Innumerable treatises on correct nutrition were written before the Tang period, but, if at all, only extracts from these works are known. The oldest surviving text dates back to the mid-seventh century. Back then, the famous doctor Sun Simiao remarked in chapter 26 of his book *Beiji qianjin yaofang*, "An appropriate diet is all that is needed to maintain

> It's only life that's limited,
> and not the longing for it. . . .
> Even the old folks try
> to escape death
> by every means possible.
> In the morning they swallow
> "sunshine essence pills,"
> in the evening, "autumnal sweet
>   alyssum."
> But instead of fostering happiness
> they just create disasters;
> because meddling with medicines
> causes countless mistakes.
>
> *Jie yao* (843)

SWEET AND SOUR RADISH (SHANXI)

Ingredients

1 medium-sized radish, peeled and cut into thin batons around 8 cm long
2 medium-sized carrots, prepared like the radish
1 tbsp salt
Marinade of 1 tbsp finely chopped ginger, 1 tbsp sugar, 1 tbsp rice vinegar, and
   1 tbsp soy sauce
5 dried chilies
Blend of 3 tbsp peanut oil and 2 tbsp sesame oil

Preparation method

1. Put the radish and carrot batons in a bowl, and salt well.
2. Drain off the resulting liquid after around 20 minutes.
3. Add the marinade and stir several times.
4. After 20 minutes, heat the oil mixture, add the chilies, and stir-fry.
5. Remove the chilies and pour the oil over the vegetables.
6. Cover before serving and leave to steep for a while.

balance and harmony. Medicines should not be taken carelessly under any circumstances." All the same, regardless of theoretical expounding other forms of prophylaxis have existed for centuries, from eating amulets to taking elixirs to prolong life.

Anything Goes?

If you are invited to dinner in China you can expect generous hospitality—anything else would be seen as an insult. A meal in company means more than indi-

Spittoon (stoneware, fifth century)

viduals eating together at the same time. It is a social event, and as such, people are expected to follow specific rituals that show appropriate respect for their elders, and politeness toward guests. This can sometimes be a strain, especially when delicacies are continually piled onto the visitors' plates and they may not know how to react. In any case, they should always sample what is offered. Guests are allowed the freedom to take their pick and savor anything placed before them—as long as something is left over, because nothing could be more embarrassing for the host than completely empty plates and bowls.

The noise level at the dinner table is generally rather loud—and not just from the lively conversation. You can also hear other sounds diners make, such as loud munching, slurping, and burping. Some of this behavior is tolerated, some is even desirable, and in certain circumstances sipping your soup demurely may be seen as a sign of dissatisfaction. This is not always the case, however, and foreigners should be careful not to show off their familiarity with Chinese culture by making a joke of burping. Remember, some of the Chinese at the table may have studied intercultural communication and could be judging their guests' behavior by Western standards. Another thing to note is that tolerance does not extend to every kind of noise: The Chinese strongly object to people blowing their noses at the table. The same applies to many other kinds of behavior, such as being too greedy, or fiddling with chopsticks. Following rules for table manners is nothing new. Even in ancient times, people were constantly being warned to watch their manners.

In any event, the dinner table is hardly dull acoustically, and can even be enhanced by the sounds associated with spitting, a longstanding, persistent habit the authorities have failed to eliminate so far. Many local governments have anti-spitting regulations that allow for draconian penalties: In Canton, a conviction for spitting can actually mean loss of the right to an apartment. At least the better kind of restaurant has become quieter since spittoons went out of fashion. Initially, the Communist regime regarded the wide-mouthed bowls

> [At a banquet], the rules of etiquette [govern] the serving of food and the hospitality offered to the guests. But as soon as the dishes are on the table, everybody should serve himself, depending on whether he prefers lean or fat food, in whole chunks, or cut up small. The best thing is to accept the guests' wishes. Why pressure them by forcing [particular morsels] on them?
>
> *Suiyuan shidan* (1790), chapter 2

> The following [sorts of behavior] are considered impolite during a meal in company: rolling the rice into balls; gulping down drinks and bolting down the food; crunching bones with the teeth; gnawing meat off the bone; taking fish from the serving plate and then putting it back; throwing bones to the dogs; sticking only to particular delicacies; ... gulping down soup greedily, or adding condiments to it; picking one's teeth; swilling down the sauces.
>
> *"Juli"* chapter in *Liji* (second century).

for spitting as beneficial for hygiene. Up into the 1980s spittoons were a feature to be seen at every state visit, and well-known politicians were proud of their accurate aim. Perhaps they were not very different from the court elite in the impe-

> People spit better over a short [distance] than a long one. But it is more virtuous not to spit at all.
>
> *Yinshan zhengyao* (1330), chapter 1

rial era, who furnished their studios and reception rooms more than a thousand years ago with perfectly molded pottery spittoons.

You should wash your hands before eating, and your mouth afterward. This brief, elegant maxim could well be an instruction from Confucius, but in fact it was Buddhist monastery dis-

cipline that developed the first hygienic standards to spread beyond court circles. The religion of Buddhism, which came from India, brought a new vision of humankind to China, and a wealth of practical knowledge and technological achievements. One consequence was a culture of bathing that was even partly accessible to the wider public. At least from the era of the Tang dynasty, various herbal mixtures for washing were added to the bath water. Alkalis were another kind of additive, including soda (although long-term use is harmful to the skin). Demand was predictably great when soaps from the West arrived on the market in the mid-nineteenth century. Not only were they much milder but they helped to reduce unpleasant body odor.

Vomiting (book illustration, 1801)

Buddhist monks also set an example of tooth cleaning by using little wooden sticks, preferably from plum tree branches, that were chewed at one end until soft and frayed. Toothpicks were known at least by the Tang period; the most precious were made of gold and silver. A kind of toothpaste made of plant and mineral substances was available. The toothbrush, which is a Chinese invention—as is dental floss—came

> Mint banishes the strong smell of fish.
>
> *Wulei xianggan zhi* (around 980), chapter 1

into use several centuries later, but remained restricted to the elite for a long period. Many people only learned of these achievements after the end of the imperial age, when modern Western hygiene began to gain ground, although not everywhere. In some regions in the 1990s, consumer acceptance of toothbrushes was below 30 percent, and in many places the decisive breakthrough only happened very recently. Before that, people used to wash their mouths out with water. Since this was not really effective, all kinds of household remedies were used to fight bad breath.

> Eating garlic causes bad breath. [To remedy this], take a mixture of ginger and jujube.
>
> *Wulei xianggan zhi* (around 980), chapter 4
>
> To prevent tooth decay and bad breath, always wash your mouth out with warm water after eating a meal.
>
> *Yinshan zhengyao* (1330), chapter 1

Bowel movements presented a different kind of olfactory challenge. A wall painting in Dunhuang dating back to the sixth century (in Cave 290 at Mogao) contains a detailed image of a person shielded by a partition crouching over a hole in the ground and defecating. The person probably felt good about the contribution, knowing the pit would be emptied later and the liquid manure used to fertilize crops in the fields. Animal farmers played their part in the circulation of dung as well: The favorite site for toilets on their land was above the pigsties.

A large section of the rural population, however, would have relieved themselves in the open air. Specially built toilet cabins were the exception rather than the rule, and structures even remotely resembling the cleanliness and splendor of the ancient Roman latrines were completely unknown in China. Fortunately, the architectural and hygienic standards of the public toilets in some big Chinese cities have improved in the past several years, but you should still be careful where you go to the lavatory, and never assume toilet paper will be provided.

In the past, many people probably avoided the lavatory because it was seen as the lair of spirits and demons. Chapter 113 of the *Fayuan zhulin*, a seventh-century Buddhist text, offered advice on proper toilet comportment, if necessary after conquering superstitious fears. It seems that snapping your fingers was the most important way to communicate during your visit to the toilet, whether to announce that you wanted to enter or to show it was occupied once you were inside. The text even prescribed the right position: squatting with your feet placed parallel to each other, without leaning against the walls, and looking straight ahead. Using too much water for washing afterward was prohibited, as was using too much soil when filling the pit to cover the defecation, and writing graffiti on the walls. Finally, according to the *Fayuan zhulin,* it was indecent for a person "to go red in the face due to holding his breath for too long."

Chapter Seven

The Tavern of Eternal Happiness

Entertaining in Style

Contrary to the widely accepted picture, the nuclear family consisting of two parents and their unmarried children has always been the basic form of communal life in China. There may have been vertically or horizontally extended families with grandparents and grandchildren, siblings, and relatives by marriage, but households seldom consisted of more than six or seven people under one roof.

The exception was the upper class, where a multigenerational household was the rule. Although a man was only allowed one wife, he could take as many concubines as he could afford. This was obligatory, in fact, for a status-conscious gentleman who wanted to keep up his reputation. The concubines were expected to establish a strict hierarchy among themselves. They were subordinate not only to their master and his wife, but also to his parents, who were highly respected. The classic compendium of social standards, the *Liji*, may have conveyed the Confucian ideal rather than the reality, but at least it gave an idea of the power constellations.

> If the son is happy with his wife but his parents do not like her, he should divorce her. [In the opposite case] he should continue the duties of marriage diligently until the end of her life.
>
> "*Neize*" chapter in the *Liji* (second century)

The family was seen as a mirror of the cosmic order that determined the decision-making power of the father and the dominance of the husband. For many centuries, lack of respect for age was seen as a moral weakness and a contravention of prevailing law. The Tang Codex listed contempt and negligence toward parents among the ten worst deeds of infamy, along with rebellion, high treason, profligacy, and incest. The privileged status of previous generations was evident in the dietary rules of antiquity. For example, the *"Neize"* chapter of the *Liji* explained that the son was expected "to pay his father an evening visit and show affection by bringing him delicious tidbits." The Liji also reported that people were often granted extra privileges on reaching middle age. By the age of 80, it seems, they were allowed to spend the whole day eating treats, and at 90, even to take meals in bed.

The dining rules allowed children a modicum of freedom: Unlike the rest of the family, their meals were not tied to set times. Assuming people could afford several meals a day, they usually ate at three different intervals: the first from 6 to 7 A.M., the second from 11 A.M. to noon, and the third from 5 to 6 P.M. In many parts of the country the traditional breakfast consists of rice porridge made by cooking the grains in large quantities of water until they disintegrate. The poetic literature sings the praises of this gruel, but to describe it as bland would really be an understatement. Flavor is generally added by a selection of extra ingredients, including roasted peanuts, fried vegetables, pickled eggs, or fish paste. Sweet variations are also common.

> I was surprised that she [Cixi] could eat anything at all, considering the quantity of sweets she had already consumed. . . . This day we had pork cooked in ten different ways. In the center of the table was a very large yellow porcelain bowl containing a chicken, a duck, and shark fins in clear soup. . . . Roast chicken and duck were also served. . . .
>
> There was another dish that Her Majesty was very fond of and that was the skin of roast pork cut into very small slices and fried until it curls up like a rasher of bacon. . . . After the meat she recommended us [three ladies-in-waiting] to eat mash from sweet corn and from tiny yellow rice seeds. There was a large variety of different breads as well. . . . Then we had sour and brined pickled vegetables, which Her Majesty enjoyed very much. Finally, there were beans and green peas, and peanuts made into cakes and served with cane syrup.
>
> Der Ling (1921), pp. 45–48

Although the morning meal had to be as nourishing as possible, the evening meal was supposed to be fairly light, unless it was a social occasion or the diners wanted to stoke up for a drinking bout afterward. Alcoholic binges sometimes lasted until dawn. Lunch was generally the main meal. The Qing court in 1903 followed this custom, and noblewomen such as the dowager empress Cixi were not an exception.

To the outside world the husband always appeared as head of the family. It was his responsibility to handle legal affairs, and he was accountable to the state if need be. Within the family he ensured, sometimes by force, that discipline was upheld as he saw fit. However, we shouldn't underestimate the wife's position in internal family conflicts, particularly if she had borne several sons. In the daily life of the upper class, male and female spheres of activity were largely separate. Early on, a passage in chapter 3.1.4 of the *Mengzi*, a work by the great Confucian thinker Mencius dating back to the third century B.C., was already advising that the domains of husband and wife "should be separated." This custom still persisted, or was revived, toward the end of the imperial age, when the Manchurian Qing dynasty tried to compensate for its lack of legitimacy by implementing Confucian principles very strictly, not least by separating the sexes during mealtimes.

Some form of communication was obviously necessary, and advice manuals for improving virtue and household tasks, including those compiled by women, urged their sisters to demonstrate great modesty

> Even at home, in her own family, a woman must neither eat at the same table nor sit in the same room with her husband. And the male children, at the age of nine or ten, are entirely separated from their sisters.
>
> John Barrow (1805), p. 142

and self-effacement, particularly in the presence of guests. "Then her husband rejoices in her capability, and the visitor bestows compliments." Around the year 780, chapters 1 and 10 of the *Nü lunyü* called, respectively, for "purity" and "chastity," but this was not always achieved, as amply illustrated by the literature, especially the novels of the late imperial period. Although sometimes exaggerated, they clearly show culinary and sexual appetites becoming intermingled. Many of these books describe real-life situations. For example, chapter 11 of the *Jin Ping Mei*, written at the end of the sixteenth century, describes the division of labor in a household where the lady of the house became ill. The first concubine had to manage the finances, and the third concubine had to take charge of the kitchen staff.

Managing the kitchen could involve a great deal of work. Banquets at a certain social level usually required careful planning from beginning to end and, if they had a political connotation, an extra helping of tact as well. Hosting a formal dinner for guests could symbolize hegemonic claims, proposals for alliances, or withdrawal of trust. This dimension of epicurean culture can be traced very far back, almost to the very point where the written Chinese tradition began. No trouble was spared for that kind of dinner. Even the ritual of invitation was highly

> From a European standpoint the dinners are very boring, not just because they last so long but mainly because women do not participate in them. In China, both women and men believe that meals taste better when they are eaten without the presence of the opposite sex.
>
> Bruno Navarra (1901), p. 324

STEAMED FISH (GUANGXI)

Ingredients

3 tbsp (150 g) ginger, cut into thin batons around half an inch (1.5 cm) long
Juice of 1 large lemon
2 tbsp peanut oil
1 tbsp sesame oil
5 thinly sliced garlic cloves
4 tbsp sesame seeds
2 tbsp soy sauce
1¾ pound (800 g) fish fillet, preferably pieces of medium thickness

Preparation method

1. Marinate the ginger in the lemon juice for around 20 minutes.
2. Fry the garlic in the oil at medium heat.
3. Fry the sesame seeds in medium hot oil, blend in the ginger and soy sauce and pour over the fish.
4. Steam for 10 to 20 minutes, depending on the thickness of the fillets, and serve immediately.

formalized and designed to impress, and spontaneity during the event itself was absolutely frowned upon. In principle, every single detail was regulated, right down to the custom of raising cups, which could escalate into a never-ending round of toasts.

At the allotted time, the [employees of the] court kitchen served beer flavored with spices. During the elaborately staged banquets for civil servants, the guests conversed and toasted each other in the palace park. The Court of Imperial Sacrifices determined the . . . hierarchy of the seating order, and the censors observed the reception throughout. . . . At the signal for a toast . . . people raised their cups, accompanied by the rhythm of string instruments.

Yalaji jiu fu (1344)

Court ranking always had to be borne in mind at official receptions, and the guests had to observe a complex code of precedence. The *Liji* devoted an entire chapter, *Yanyi*, to the relevant regulations, laying down rules on matters such as the seating order, the sequence of toasts and the size of the meat helpings. However, these guidelines do not always seem to have been followed to the letter, at least in relation to the presumed presence of the emperor. As far back as we can discover, the emperor did not attend the banquet in person, but sent a representative instead. While the guests dined in stately halls, the "sons of heaven," who were elevated above the mortal sphere, usually ate meals in their private quarters, surrounded only by a few courtiers who were humbly obliged to stand the whole time, even if they were allowed to eat the food.

In 1901, after living in China for twenty years, Bruno Navarra, former editor in chief of the *Ostasiatischer Lloyd* in Shanghai, claimed that Chinese family relations generally inhibited "social gatherings from taking place in people's homes" (pp. 234–235). He was obviously unaware of the distance maintained between foreigners and the indigenous populace because,

> In the banqueting hall, breakfast was served in the Manchu style. Since her Majesty (Cixi) and the Emperor (Guangxu) never ate with guests, Madame Plançon [the wife of the Russian envoy] was escorted to the table by the imperial princess and the ladies in waiting.
>
> Der Ling (1912), p. 57

contrary to his opinion, the Chinese did invite guests for meals at home, and not only in restaurants. It is true that city dwellers were more likely to invite visitors to dine in restaurants than in Europe, but this was hardly the rule, whether for a formal occasion, a family celebration, or a booze-up.

Finally, there were two other options: first, erecting a tent and hiring a restaurant company, the equivalent of a modern catering firm; second, the communal picnic that was described by poets as early as the Tang period, and was a popular subject for painters over the centuries.

> Sloppiness is forbidden when your betters come to call. First of all, you must put out the chairs for the esteemed guests, spread the tablecloths, arrange the umbrellas, and set out the tobacco goods; then come the three bows and the hundred greetings. But what is actually the point of these stupid conventions if people can relax at home with a nice meal or a literary drinks party? . . . However, certain formalities cannot be avoided, even for birthdays or wedding celebrations within the family circle, when five or six tables are set up and extra kitchen help is hired.
>
> Suiyuan shidan (1790), chapter 2

Picnicking with Ancestors

People in China, as elsewhere, needed celebrations now and then to break up the routine of daily life. The main occasions were the rites of passage, including birth, naming, coming-of-age, passing examinations, marriage and death, and the festivals at fixed points in the yearly calendar. Although they might involve enormous effort, the money was not wasted. Ultimately, those who showed generosity were strengthening social bonds and securing their status in society.

Picnic (book illustration, 1801)

Many traditions have not survived the deformations of the twentieth century, but this does not mean rituals no longer play a part in Chinese life—and what all these rituals have in common is eating well and drinking merrily.

Infant mortality was high. Aside from the sickness and epidemics that caused early death, there was the so-called baby bath, a euphemism for drowning unwanted infants, particularly girls. A bath also marked a key moment in the early life of a wanted child: the ceremonial first haircut and washing that took place a month after the birth. Aromatic substances were often added to the bath water, and in some regions, food as well, which young women fished out after bathing and ate to improve their own childbearing chances. The postpartum ceremony, which ended with a communal meal, marked the child's increasing integration into the family and was followed by ceremonies after 100 days and after one year. Otherwise birthdays were generally not lavishly celebrated, at least until the age of fifty. Even then, the favorite dish at the celebrations was noodles whose length was equated with the lifespan of the birthday person, which meant nobody was allowed to cut them.

The bridal couple sealed the marriage pact by sharing a drink. In fact, drinking alcohol played a major role throughout the wedding celebrations. While elaborate cooking underlined the host's purchasing power, simple dishes were also an essential part of the menu because of their symbolic effect. This has hardly changed over the centuries. Lotus nuts are still served to symbolize a lasting relationship, indicated by a homophonous term (*lian*). Peanuts, known as the "fruit of long life" (*changshengguo*), are nearly always on the table. Moreover, the second character (*sheng*), meaning "to bring forth," expresses hope that the union will soon be blessed with a child. Sources such as guidelines laid down over 800 years ago reveal that, however informal, the wedding was governed by detailed lists of rules, from hiring the marriage bro-

ker to introducing the couple to their re-
spective parents-in-law. Relics of customs
once confined to the upper class can still
be found in China today, particularly in
rural areas.

The methods of dealing with the deceased sometimes resemble administrative directives, and some documents from
the Han period really make burials seem
like a bureaucratic procedure. This applies especially to the choice and number
of burial offerings, which often included
foods. There is no firm evidence for the
common assumption that the food deposited in the grave was intended
to facilitate the deceased person's journey to the nether world. The key
issues were showing appropriate honor to the interred person, docu-
menting his or her rank, and describing his or her personality. It is still
largely unclear to whom the custom of food offerings was addressed,
but there are at least two possibilities: the realm of the dead, where
would-be entrants could only win appropriate status by arriving with
substantial material trappings, or the world of the living, where the surviving relatives and friends used the occasion to demonstrate their pres-
tige. The funeral feast, which, like the food offerings, was sometimes
held at the graveside in ancient times, should be seen in this context
as well. The result was that the immedi-
ate survivors were more restrained in eating, and only the deceased person's wider
circle could feast freely.

The end of the mourning period does
not mean a definitive break with the ties
to the deceased. Three ceremonies at vari-
ous points in the year are dedicated to the dead; the most important is
Remembrance Day for the Dead (*qingmingjie*), which falls on April 4
or 5. People gather at the graves, clean and decorate them, make offerings to their ancestors, and finally eat a meal, as if sharing with their
forefathers. This is a relatively informal picnic. In the Song era people
ate jujube cakes, salted duck's eggs, candied fruits, and various milk
products. Today's picnic basket is more likely to contain glutinous rice
balls and lotus roots.

> On the day at the appropriate time her family provides a large meal and many jugs of beer . . . , the bride bows, takes the food and serves it to her parents-in-law. . . . When they have finished eating she clears up, and the servants serve out the remaining food in the other rooms. Then she eats from the food left over by her mother-in-law, and her companions take what her father-in-law left. Finally, the bridegroom's entourage dines on what the bride has left uneaten.
>
> *Jiali* (around 1190), chapter 3

> As for the gentleman in mourning, delicious food he eats is not tasty, music he hears does not make him happy, and he cannot live at ease.
>
> *Lunyu* (around 450 B.C.), chapter 17

The two other annual occasions for remembering the dead have less impact on everyday life. They are not tied to specific dates in the Gregorian calendar (which has been in force since the beginning of the Republic): They occur on the fifteenth day of the seventh month and the first day of the tenth month, which means they follow the lunisolar calendar, like all the other traditional festivals. According to this, the New Year normally falls on the second new moon after the winter solstice in the period between January 21 and February 21. The family gathers in advance for a festive meal on the evening before and, if affordable, the menu has to include a fish dish. Usually this is not completely eaten, which is supposed to express the wish for continuing prosperity, a symbolic gesture that transposes the homophony of "fish" and "abundance" (*yu* in each case) into a culinary setting.

> Little cakes were baked to be set out in front of the Buddhas and ancestor charts during the New Year. We went into a room specially arranged for this, and the eunuchs brought the ingredients: rice flour, sugar, and yeast. They were mixed into a dough, and steamed. The higher the rice cake rises, the more joy it brings to the gods and the fortunate people who make it. Her Majesty made the first cake herself, with great success, and we congratulated her.
>
> Der Ling (1912), pp. 251–52

Similarity in pronunciation is also the reason that chicken and hair weed (a cyanobacterium from the *Nostoc* species) are popular dishes during the days of the New Year feast: Their phonetic equivalents promise happiness (*ji*) and increased wealth (*facai*). Finally, the New Year cake made of glutinous rice (*niangao*) has positive connotations as well: A homophone of the second character, *gao*, means "enhancement," which is ideal for evoking associations with the quality of living standards. Other common foods at the New Year include peanuts and dumplings (*jiaozi*), which again imply wealth with their vague resemblance to the silver bars used as currency in the imperial period.

As we know, these wishes don't always come true, and not everybody in the population benefits, even in the present phase of economic prosperity. Large numbers of people have very limited opportunities to enjoy the attractions of the New Year season to the full. Still, there is an enormous difference nowadays compared with previous periods when the New Year celebrations were the only occasion for many people to bring a little variety into their usual monotonous diet. Incidentally, the meals were not only intended to fill the belly; they were also used for ritual communication with ancestors and making offerings to various gods.

The New Year festivities usually taper off into a relatively quiet phase and a temporary return to everyday life before reaching their finale with the exuberant Lantern Festival on the fifteenth day of the first month. The Chinese treat themselves to the typical rice balls for this festival, often filled with bean paste or other sweet things. Some revelers consume large quantities of alcohol. In the Tang era the celebrations were like a carnival that lasted over three nights and always raised the suspicions of the authorities, who were concerned about keeping up moral standards. Some moral apostles took the opportunity to make petitions to the throne complaining about the blurring of social status distinctions, loose behavior between the sexes, immoderate eating and drinking, people squandering their worldly goods, and the temporary increase in crime.

> The father wrapped the vegetarian filling in the dumplings [*jiaozi*] alone. He was nervous: this task was part of the family tradition that required making an offering to the Buddha on the evening before the New Year's festival while saving pork at the same time. The offerings had to be of the best quality. This meant the dumplings had to be particularly small, with the edges pressed together firmly with artistic skill, for badly prepared items would bring no luck.
>
> *Zhenghongqi xia* (around 1965), chapter 5

These admonitions were almost useless. In the end, the court also enjoyed itself, and the ladies-in-waiting in particular were said to plunge into the fun exuberantly. Enthusiasm for the Lantern Festival continued until the eleventh century, when the gates of the brightly lit imperial palace in Hangzhou were actually opened for an elect group of revelers after the populace had been entertained the whole day with performances by musicians, dancers, and acrobats. The tradition ended after the capital's enforced move to Kaifeng when, in the face of the latent threat on the country's borders, the ritual elements of the festival began to dominate again and the city's inhabitants were only allowed to appear in stiff jubilatory poses.

After that, other pleasures became more popular, especially the nationwide dragon boat races held on the fifth day of the fifth month. They were generally believed to originate with the quest for the body of Qu Yuan, a loyal minister who fell into disfavor nonetheless and is reputed to have drowned himself in Milo in 295 B.C. However, aside from the lengthy time gap between the alleged suicide and the initiation of the boating contests, there is justified skepticism about the idea that men who fell into the water during the races were once regarded as sacrifices to the river god. The same objection applies to the related interpretation of *zongzi,* the delicacies now eaten on that day. *Zongzi* are glutinous rice dumplings usually wrapped in bamboo or lotus leaves, and nearly every family has its own recipe for the filling. In some regions of the country, salted duck's eggs, candied fruits, and cakes made of mung bean flour are also eaten on Dragon Boat Day.

Although the particularly clear full moon on the fifteenth day of the eighth month had always been admired, it was in the Song period that the custom was established of partying on that night with relatives and friends into the small hours. The celebrations included eating moon cakes baked in typically round form with a wide variety of fillings. They are still very popular today. The full moon festival (*zhongqiujie*) focuses on familial happiness, fertility, glorification of nature, and a touch of romanticism. It occurs between two other festivals: the celebrations on the seventh day of the seventh month (*qixijie*), and the ninth day of the ninth month (*chongyangjie*). Food plays a less important role in these two festivals; during the latter, the traditional drink is chrysanthemum wine, made from a rice wine base and mixed with the flowers. Lychees and Black Mondo grass (radix *Ophiogonis* sp.) are often added for extra flavor.

In the Han period, the twelfth month was still marked by extensive ritual sacrifices, but little remains of that, and the name (*la*) is the last surviving reminder of the ancient origins of the festivities on the eighth day. Only the Buddhist monasteries really celebrate this date, because of its connection with the enlightenment of their religious founder, Shakyamuni. Most people celebrate simply with a modest festive meal of rice porridge with nuts and dried fruit. Finally, the twenty-third or twenty-fourth day is dedicated to the Lord of the Hearth, but the rites associated with this are basically to prepare for the New Year.

Business and Pleasure

Before the Tang era, the best places for city dwellers wanting to dine out were the markets and their surrounding neighborhoods. This was where most of the bars, teahouses, and inns were located; this was the place for refreshment, entertainment, and accommodations. There were already some restaurants in residential areas, but commercial eating places throughout urban space only became widespread under the Song dynasty. By the beginning of the twelfth century, the capital, Kaifeng, housed at least a dozen entertainment districts crowded with theatres, restaurants, and brothels.

At that time there were seventy-two licensed large taverns and restaurants alone in Kaifeng; by paying a heavy pre-tax they obtained the right to sell their beer to smaller pubs. One firm may have supplied up 3,000 subcontractors, which suggests an impressive concentration of taverns. Still, it must have paid off for the landlords: According to chapter 2 of the *Dongjing meng Hua lu*, customers crowded in "day and night, undeterred by storms, rain, or hot or cold weather." The enormous number of establishments in the Song metropolis gave rise to a corresponding variety of tavern names. A fair number were called after the owner or cook, such as Lucky Li's, Fat Huang's, or Smart Zhang's. In addition to the aforementioned Voluptuous Pleasures, restaurants with names such as Harmonious Bliss, Fun and Games, Good Companions, and Enduring Happiness promised a congenial atmosphere. People could also meet up at the Immortals' Meeting-Place or the Cool Breeze.

The main features of cooking in the capital were, first, the diverse kinds of inspiration from all the country's regions, and second, that there was no chance for any of the short-lived fashion fads that kept appearing to get established on a long-term basis. Landlords who came to the capital from other places gradually loosened their ties to their home regions, and the dividing lines between culinary traditions became blurred. However, a small group of restaurants made their name with regional specialties, and from the Song period onward a growing number of eating places served only vegetarian dishes.

Some well-known restaurants could seat up to a 1,000 people and offered an enormous choice of dishes on the menu. Men Yuanlao's recollections, compiled in chapter 2 of *Dongjing meng Hua lu*, refer to more than fifty different delicacies prepared in the kitchen of a fancy restaurant at the beginning of the twelfth century, including twice-cooked shark,

> In the capital, the entrances to the taverns are [marked] by gates decorated with welcoming garlands. Upon entering the Ren family's restaurant, you come directly to a central corridor a hundred paces long. The two courtyards to the north and south are each surrounded by two-story galleries with small rooms leading off them. At dusk the lamps shine from all sides, and hundreds of beautifully dolled up hostesses wait in the central corridor for the guests to call them. . . . The Alum Inn was later renamed "Voluptuous Pleasures." During the Xuanhe era [1119–1125], it was rebuilt as a complex of five three-story houses with interconnecting walkways with balustrades. Light and dark areas blend into each other; the bead curtains and plaques at the doors are illuminated with bright light.
>
> *Dongjing meng Hua lu* (1148), chapter 2

deep-fried crawfish, duck cut in thin strips, braised lamb, fried rabbit, flying fox fish, tripe cooked in beer, and quail soup. There were female as well as male waiters. The young boys who helped serve were colloquially addressed as "venerable uncle," but this was a jokey euphemism rather than a mark of respect. In fact, the service staff certainly deserved appreciation, because some pampered guests were not easy to please.

Orders are dealt with immediately. If the food doesn't taste right, [the guest can] complain and get another dish instead.

People in the metropolis are extravagant and thoughtless; . . . every guest wants something different. . . . Customers complain to the host about even the smallest slip, whereupon the host scolds the waiter or docks some of his pay; at worst he even risks being sacked.

Dongjing meng Hua lu (1148), chapters 2 and 4

The eating places also offered a big choice of specialties made off the premises. Hawkers went through the rooms selling lamb hock, ginger prawns, or lotus leaf wraps. Their biggest attraction was a wide variety of fresh, bottled, dried, and candied fruit, as well as nuts and sweets such as the famous Lion Toffees from Sichuan. They also provided services such as running errands, doing shopping, or finding staff for hire. Finally, people known as "table scroungers" serenaded from table to table, hoping the guests would be generous.

According to contemporary historical accounts, food from the smaller establishments and from street traders was relatively inexpensive. No dish cost more than 15 *wen* (a *wen* was a coin made of copper, lead, and tin alloy, and threaded on string through a hole in the middle). All the reports were by members of the upper class, however, and ordinary people probably saw things differently. By comparison, an adult resident of the poorhouse received around 125 g of rice and beans daily and 10 *wen* in cash. Customers in the better restaurants could pay a fortune for meals, nor were the drinks cheap. A jug of Silver Bottle beer in the Immortals' Meeting-Place tavern could cost 72 *wen*, and Lamb Beer cost as much as 81 *wen*.

Things became really pricey for men visiting places that provided the company of bar girls, who generally demanded only the best food and drink. Patrons of superior establishments were rewarded with a lavish entertainment program. Added benefits usually included tasteful surroundings, cultivated conversation, and excellent manners. Frequently more was involved than merely satisfying intellectual and epicurean desires, and the guests made good use of the private rooms. This often led to a happy union of the enterprises of gastronomy and prostitution

Rooftop banquet (book illustration, 1801)

> [Going towards the inner courtyard], you find one small room after another. . . . Each room has curtains on the windows. The hostesses hired for singing and distraction do a good job.
>
> *Dongjing meng Hua lu* (1148), chapter 2

under one roof—much to the gratification of the treasury department, which profited from the extra tax revenues this alliance generated.

The service was exquisite, as was the tableware used for serving the food and drink. The luxurious atmosphere of these establishments drew many regular customers. One of them, a high-ranking court official named Lu Zongdao (966–1029), is recorded as saying that because his home environment was not impressive enough,

Waitress with tray (668)

he invited his guests to meet him in the Good Companions. Most of the clientele were members of the educated elite, such as public servants, scholars, artists, and students; but merchants, men of leisure, and snobs were also well represented.

Anyway, the distinctions between these groups were sometimes blurred, and according to the *Shang huangdi wan yan shu*, which appeared in 1058, public servants could probably only afford these pleasures regularly if they received bribes of "money and gifts." When ordering, for instance, it was important to observe particular conventions, and anybody ignoring them was exposed to the mockery of insiders, who enjoyed poking fun at greenhorns.

Aside from the selection of beverages, teahouses were not very different from other catering establishments. People gathered there mainly to make business deals, enjoy cultivated conversation, and meet prostitutes. In the Song era, unlike other periods, women may also have been accepted as guests, although there is little remaining evidence of this. The food consisted mainly of snacks, including the filled dumplings known in the West by their Cantonese name, *dim sum* (or *dianxin* in Mandarin), which means "little morsels the heart desires." Incidentally, many teahouses promoted art in the form of exhibitions of the latest picture scrolls by well-known artists, or performances of inspiring music.

> My family isn't rich, and I don't have any [good] tableware. But bars and restaurants are nicely furnished and give their customers the feeling of being at home. That's why I invite my friends there for a beer when they visit here, far away from home.
>
> Lu Zongdao, cited in *Guitianlu* (1067), chapter 1

A large part of the population probably never set foot in a posh restaurant or tavern, and many people had so little money to spare that even going to simple establishments was out of the question. If they wanted to eat out decently, the huge number of cook shops offered a cheap alternative. In Kaifeng, most of the small taverns and booths specialized in foods such as filled dumplings, pumpkin soup, or flat bread.

> In the Artificial Mountain teahouse, there are caves and bridges [depicting the world] of the immortals. Young men and women often come here at night to drink tea.
>
> *Dongjing meng Hua lu* (1148), chapter 2

Hawkers also stocked up there with wares to resell later on the streets. Sometimes, however, they let the customer gamble for a meal by tossing a coin to see whether he would pay the price but go away empty-handed and hungry, or whether he would get the meal for free.

What did people of bygone ages do when they had to stay away from home overnight? Where did the public official go for food, drink, and lodgings when he was on a service trip, or the businessman working away from home, or pious believers on a pilgrimage? Chapter 3 of the *Dongjing meng Hua lu* mentions innumerable inns in Kaifeng, but only a few hotels, including the Radiant Splendor and the Peerless, although it is not clear whether the latter's name referred to the establishment's quality or its prices.

Travel was difficult in those days, and the choice of accommodation was limited. The only relatively dense net of state-owned inns and posting houses was found along the arterial routes, but they were reserved for public officials, at least in principle. From the Ming dynasty onward, similar restrictions applied to staying in the branch offices of the guilds, which were active on a transregional basis by then. Only registered members were permitted to stay overnight at these offices, to deposit their wares and conduct their monetary transactions there. The *huiguan* (conference houses) were formally separate from the guilds, but actually

FRIED RICE (ZHEJIANG, JIANGSU)

Ingredients

1 cup (250 g) rice
2 eggs
3 sliced scallions
1 red pepper, diced, around ¼ inch (0.5 × 0.5 cm)
1 large carrot, diced, around ¼ inch (0.5 × 0.5 cm)
1 tbsp finely chopped garlic
1 tbsp finely chopped ginger
⅓ oz (10 g) dried shiitake mushrooms; soak in warm water for 30 minutes, then
    remove the stalks and chop finely
4 oz (100 g) bamboo shoots, diced, around ¼ inch (0.5 × 0.5 cm)
5 oz (150 g) boiled ham, diced, around ¼ inch (0.5 × 0.5 cm)
5 oz (150 g) small prawns (shelled and deveined), poached
2 tbsp soy sauce
2 tbsp rice wine
2 tbsp chicken stock
1 tsp salt
½ tsp pepper

Preparation method

1. Cook the rice (which swells to almost three times its original weight); this can
   be done a day in advance.
2. Beat the eggs, pour them into a pan with heated peanut oil and make a thin
   omelet, then cut into small squares.
3. Stir-fry the scallions, pepper, and carrots in peanut oil.
4. Add the garlic, ginger, and shiitake mushrooms, and fry together for two
   minutes; remove, and keep warm.
5. Stir-fry the bamboo shoots, ham, and prawns in some peanut oil; keep warm.
6. Stir-fry the rice in peanut oil, add all the warm ingredients, and the egg, soy
   sauce, chicken stock, and rice wine, and stir in well.
7. Season with salt and pepper.

closely interconnected. They were meeting-places for people who came from the same region and wanted to enjoy cooking and an atmosphere that reminded them of home. Buddhist and Daoist monasteries that offered shelter, particularly in the countryside, had a long tradition of being much more generous, but did not always welcome visitors warmly. As the *Wanghuailu*, a practical manual compiled in around 1070, noted, another option was to carry a tent, along with adequate provisions, mainly dried meat, dried vegetables, and bakery goods.

Finally, many people stayed in private lodgings such as the homes of relatives or business partners, or even with total strangers who could be persuaded to provide bed and board for a small fee. Demand for food and lodgings rose considerably from the fifteenth century on. Travel was increasingly seen as an "art," and at times there was a big stream of tourists across the country. This barely had an effect on the infrastructure, however: Suspicion of strangers grew rather than decreasing, and comfort remained at modest levels. Europeans who wanted to travel around outside the major cities had to get accustomed to this.

> 18th day of the 4th month: The monastery was extremely poor, and the monks behaved in a vulgar, uncouth manner. – 19th day of the 4th month: The monks were simple souls, and reacted nervously when they realized we were visiting. – 20th day of the 4th month: Our host had the heart of a bandit and cheated people. – 21st day of the 4th month: When the two monks saw we were coming to stay as guests they sent us away several times with vile curses. After we finally managed to get in to the monastery . . . their attitude changed, and they prepared noodles for us visiting monks with their own hands.
>
> Excerpts from *Nittō gubō junrei kōki*, the diary of the Japanese monk Ennin (840)

A Really Important Place

Leaving aside the suburbs, Beijing was divided into three parts under the Qin dynasty. In the center was the Imperial Palace district (1), which was shielded from the outside world and surrounded on all four sides by the Manchurian quarters (2) named after the Eight Banners. The

> In this country, they invariably shut their doors against a stranger. What they call inns are mean hovels . . . where, perhaps, a traveller may procure his cup of tea for a piece of copper money, and permission to pass the night.
>
> John Barrow (1805), p. 283

Chinese lived in five adjacent city districts in the south (3). According to the 1903 census, in these areas alone there were 265 temples, 275 inns, 301 hotels, 247 restaurants, and 247 teahouses. Admittedly, they were heavily outnumbered by the opium dens (699) and brothels (308).

In those days Peking Duck was only found on the menu of a few specialized restaurants. This superb dish was probably borrowed from the court kitchen under the previous dynasty, the Ming, but the records for this period are not really clear, although the renowned Bianyifan restaurant claims to have served this as a specialty as early as 1416. Historically, the tradition can only be traced back to the mid-nineteenth century, when part of the firm split off and set up on its own. This was the beginning of the great rival enterprise, the Quanjude, which is still operating as an international concern with more than fifty branches. Its main restaurant boasts more than forty rooms and can cater for up to 5,000 customers a day, including members of important foreign delegations, and endless hordes of tourists.

Beijing residents usually go out to eat duck—most of them would never dream of roasting the bird in their own kitchen. The common cooking method today requires a big purpose-built stove, preferably heated with fruit tree wood to obtain the desired flavor. After the fire has died down, the bird is hung as near to the middle of the room as possible to expose it to the high temperature from all sides and to limit the cooking time to around a half to three quarters of an hour. An alternative method involves laying the roasting duck on a metal grid, but attempts to emulate the traditional recipe in an ordinary oven are usually disappointing, especially if you have had the chance to enjoy the "original" version.

Peking Duck is not only the name of the dish, but also the name of the bird used to make it, a white-feathered descendant of the mallard (*Anas platyrhynchos domestica*) that was successfully bred for centuries in the area around the capital. The birds have an average "life expectancy" of a little over sixty days, of which the first third are spent in free range. Then the fattening begins, with four feeds a day and substantial restriction of movement, which is supposed to yield the right relation between tender flesh, an even layer of fat, and a thin skin.

To achieve the famous crust at the end of cooking, the cooks make a small cut in the duck's skin after slaughtering, and pump air in, loosening the skin carefully from the flesh so that it only stays firmly connected at a few points. Then they scald the duck, brush it with a sugar solution, and leave it to dry for several hours before putting it in the stove.

The cooked bird is usually carved by specialized cooks who remove the skin at incredible speed and cut it, with the outer layer of meat, into more than 100 strips. The pieces are wrapped in small pancakes, together with fine strips of scallion and cucumber, and delicate plum or bean sauce. Exceptionally, you are allowed to eat the pancakes with your hands. The duck's heart, liver, gizzard, tongue, wings, and feet webbing are usually served separately; the rest of the bird is used as the basis for a soup the waiters serve right at the end.

MONGOLIAN HOT POT (MONGOLIA, BEIJING)

Ingredients

1 tbsp (50 g) chopped scallions
1 tbsp (50 g) chopped coriander leaves
1 tbsp (50 g) chopped ginger
1 tbsp (50 g) chopped garlic
3½ tbsp. (50 ml) soy sauce
3½ tbsp. (50 ml) rice vinegar
3½ tbsp. (50 ml) chili sauce
8 cups (2 L) chicken stock (preferably homemade)
2 lbs (1 kg) lamb, very finely sliced (slicing is easiest when the meat is still frozen)
8 oz (200 g) sliced celery sticks
8 oz (200 g) bok choy, cut into strips
8 oz (200 g) spinach
2 oz (50 g) glass noodles

Preparation method

1. Place the scallions, coriander leaves, ginger, garlic, soy sauce, rice vinegar, and chili sauce in small bowls on the dining table for each guest to mix individual dips.
2. Bring the stock to the boil in the hot pot (or a classic fondue pot) and briefly cook a small portion (a quarter at most) of the meat and vegetables in it.
3. Fish the pieces of food out with wooden chopsticks or little wire baskets and eat with the dips.
4. Repeat the cooking several times, adding small helpings of meat and vegetables each time.
5. When all the meat and vegetables are used up, add the glass noodles and serve in soup bowls with the broth.

Note: This hot pot has countless variations, including vegetarian and seafood recipes.

This is regarded as a particular delicacy, like the broth left over from a Mongolian hot pot, another dish that is eaten only in company. This also requires a special cooker. Today it is mainly heated by electricity or by using lighting gel, but it was originally charcoal-fired. The chimney in the middle grew out of the need for a smoke outlet and helps ensure that the heat is evenly distributed in the revolving pot.

The attraction, if any, of the eating-places in Beijing under the Qing was due more to the quality of the cooking than to their architecture or interior decor. By contrast, the establishments in the south were often more brightly decorated. There were also floating restaurants in places such as the West Lake in Hangzhou, or the waterways of Yangzhou, where the colorful pleasure craft usually sailed in convoys. According to chapter 11 of the *Yangzhou hufang lu*, a travel guide published in 1795, most of the boats were not equipped with a fully functioning galley, and meals had to be ordered in advance from local caterers. Kitchen crews for preparing specialties on board could only be hired in exceptional cases. There was also on-board musical entertainment, and the alcoholic beverages were kept ready on dinghies till required. The service on some of the amusement boats is said to have been exquisite and exclusive, with special attention from the female staff included. At that time the gourmet aspect of the pleasure boats was obviously a side issue in Canton.

While most teahouses were still luxurious meeting places for the upper class in the Song period, a kind of democratization gradually developed under later dynasties. Critical intellectuals could rub shoulders with prosperous merchants, and ambitious officials could meet down-at-the-heels actors. The quiet, reserved customer came here for his cheap cup of tea as well as the pushy chatterbox, and those who could afford it sampled one of the delicious snacks. Guests sat together listening to professional storytellers, watching theater performances, or listening to music recitals, and in between they discussed, argued, declaimed, and gossiped with equal passion.

SESAME BALLS

Ingredients

scant 1 cup (300 g) glutinous rice flour
10 oz (300 g) lotus paste
2 oz (50 g) sesame seeds
Oil for deep frying

Preparation Method

1. Combine the flour smoothly with around ½ cup (120 ml) of hot water and leave to stand for a few minutes; then knead firmly until the dough is stretchy.
2. Shape the dough into ropes around 2 inches in diameter, cut into 12 slices, and roll them out until the diameter has roughly doubled in size.
3. Put a dab of lotus paste in the center of the dough rounds and shape into little balls.
4. Moisten them slightly with water, and roll in the sesame seeds.
5. Fry the balls at medium heat until golden brown, then quickly remove and serve.

In 1957, a year before the Great Leap Forward, there were no fewer than 443 teahouses in Chengdu, with seating for more than 50,000 customers. In relation to the population at the time, this meant sixty-five seats for every 1,000 residents. In the same year, in Beijing, Lao She finished writing his theater play "The Teahouse" (*Chaguan*), a peerless literary representation of the atmosphere in a tavern where people eat, drink, talk, gamble, and argue. Victimized and bullied by fanatical youngsters, the author committed suicide in 1966, shortly after the beginning of the Cultural Revolution. Only a short time later, the last teahouses were obliged to close. There was no place for them any longer in an age when tradition was regarded as a reactionary provocation.

Lao She was rehabilitated in 1978, and a Beijing teahouse was named after him in 1988. One of around 400 that reappeared in the capital, today it presents opera, shadow play, and acrobatics, and is quite unique as a cultural center. This is on a very high level (with prices to match), but the pseudo-historical atmosphere makes it hard to imagine the time the writer described so vividly back in the 1950s. The charm has gone, and it is more likely to attract tourists than local people. Frankly, I think Lao She wouldn't have felt comfortable there.

> Every day he got up very early to go to the teahouse, where he sat for hours over his bowl of tea. A bowl cost two *fen* (cents) in the small taverns in the capital, Beijing. . . . Customers who brought their own tea leaves only had to pay one *fen* [for the hot water].
>
> *Ershinian mudu gui xianzhuang* (1906–1910), chapter 6

> The Teahouse (*Chaguan*). From directions for Act One
>
> . . . the teahouse was an important institution of those times, a place where people came to transact business, or simply to while away the time.
> In teahouses one could hear the most absurd stories, such as how in a certain place a huge spider had turned into a demon and was then struck by lightning. One could also come in contact with the strangest views; for example, that foreign troops could be prevented from landing by building a Great Wall along the sea coast. Here one might also hear about the latest tune composed by some Beijing Opera star, or the best way to prepare opium. In the teahouse one might also see rare art objects newly acquired by some patron—a jade fan pendant, recently unearthed, or a three color glazed snuff bottle (. . .)
>
> Lao She. *The Teahouse. A Play in Three Acts.* Translated by John Howard-Gibbon. Beijing: The Chinese University Press, 2004, p. 12.

Chapter Eight

Epilogue

Fast Food for Little Emperors

Chinese food culture was heavily influenced from abroad several times in the country's history. Probably the biggest impact occurred under the Tang dynasty, when the empire was open to new impulses in almost every sphere of cultural activity and to changes in everyday life, whether fashion or eating habits. During that period a large variety of previously unknown ingredients reached the Middle Kingdom by the Silk Road. Drinking wine from grapes became increasingly popular, and consumption of tea became ritualized. Dietary rules based on medical theories and religious beliefs were refined in new ways. Complex ideas about eating and drinking developed, and the literary approach to culinary culture became correspondingly sophisticated.

> *Dialogue while tasting top-fermented dark beer:* "Ugh, what kind of black brew is this? It looks like medicine! And that foam on top! You can't drink it—not on your life!"
>
> – "But it really tastes good, [especially if] you gulp down the liquid and foam together."
>
> – "It's so bitter, it must be medicine."
>
> *Xin shitou ji* (1905), chapter 9

The second major foreign impact began in the nineteenth century and has basically lasted until the present. Like the first, it traveled from West to East; this time, however, it originated in Europe and America rather than in other regions of Asia. The first restaurants in China specializing in French and English cuisine opened in the 1860s, but it would take another two decades for the indigenous Chinese upper class to welcome them enthusiastically. The atmosphere of these eating-places was often more attractive than the food or drink available, which

礼貌待客 热情周到 文明经商

Service with a smile (propaganda poster, 1983)

was largely prepared by Cantonese cooks, even in the north of the country, and frequently relied on imported conserves, at least to begin with.

Although the combination of different flavors and cooking methods may have forced cooks to compromise, it also gave them the chance to develop their creativity. This had its effect on menu design as well. Menus were commonplace by the end of the nineteenth century, making it easier for customers to order dishes individually. Sometimes the calligraphy on the menu was more elaborate than the cooking in the kitchen.

Today you can eat excellent French or Italian food in China's main cities. Although many exotic foods are still imported, even delicacies such as *foie gras* are now being produced locally. Some premier restaurants also borrow from foreign sources such as German cuisine, although this is usually confined to traditional foods like sausage and pork knuckle, and the décor is likely to match. Many Chinese today associate Western lifestyle with wine and cheese, and consumption of these products is rising enormously, despite the widespread incidence of genetic intolerance.

Milk products originally played a major role only in the country's northern and western border zones. There were two main reasons for this: First, these areas were inhabited by groups practicing pastoral farming, such as the Mongol, Kazakh, and Kyrgyz populations that still live there. Second, the vast majority of Han suffer from lactose intolerance. Nevertheless, many people, particularly in the big cities, are influenced by Western lifestyles and want their diet to include milk, yoghurt, and cheese. This has become easier because lactose-free (and therefore tolerable) fermented dairy products are increasingly dominating the market. The amount of dairy has increased fourfold in the past ten years and is currently more than 40 million metric tons, making China the third largest producer of dairy products worldwide. Still, the demand is so great that additional imports are necessary. Given the vast demographic, we can get a clearer picture by looking at comparative figures based on per capita consumption: For instance, China's dairy consumption is roughly equivalent to 12 percent of the U.S. consumption. Most of the milk in China is processed into fresh dairy products. Cheese, on the other hand, is largely imported, with three quarters of the imports coming from Australia and New Zealand. Big supermarkets also stock Italian Parmesan, Dutch Gouda, Swiss Gruyère, and French Roquefort.

Processing dough (watercolor, around 1870)

China once had an important tradition of viticulture, but this was largely forgotten in the nineteenth century, and a revival attempt toward the end of the imperial period failed to achieve lasting results. There has only been a noticeable improvement in the quantity and quality of imported wine, as well as homegrown varieties, over the past twenty years. In any case, the days when Great Wall wine hardly faced any competition in Chinese stores are definitely over. Top-quality brands are increasingly being produced with international cooperation, although, for the most part, only the newly prosperous class can afford them. Yet a fat wallet does not always mean specialist knowledge—or at least, this is suggested by the habit one occasionally sees of mixing wine into Coca-Cola cocktails. Meanwhile, another, nicer custom is coming into vogue: that of giving a fine wine as a gift, even at the risk of its never being drunk, or being opened much too late.

Mineral water, lemonade, and other fizzy drinks have been sold in China since the 1860s. Coca-Cola started trying to conquer the Chinese market in 1918, but it took nine years until the first bottling in Shanghai. This success did not hold for long: The Communists' accession to power was followed by a long dry period, and Coca-Cola was only able to re-establish itself in China after the end of the Cultural Revolution. It has since achieved a market share almost double that of its perennial competitor, Pepsi. Coca-Cola was the main sponsor of the 2008 Olympic Games in Beijing and tried to strengthen its market presence in the following year, but the authorities eventually refused it permission to take over Huiyuan, the biggest domestic juice manufacturer. Incidentally, the Chinese do not always drink their Coke chilled: A popular remedy for a head cold is to add ginger and drink it as hot as possible.

The opening of McDonald's first restaurant in China in 1992 was a major event. It was the biggest branch the fast food chain had ever set up worldwide, serving up to 40,000 customers on the opening day in Beijing. Twenty years later, there were around 1,400 branches nationwide. Still, that was not enough to overtake Kentucky Fried Chicken (KFC), which is the market leader among Western fast food chains in China and looks set to remain so for a long time to come. This is due to the enduring popularity of chicken, as well as the remarkable flexibility that enables KFC to adapt to indigenous food tastes. Perhaps only Pizza Hut matches this degree of ingenuity: The type of pizza they serve in China has even less in common with the Italian product than the U.S. variety.

Western firms have demonstrated their adaptive capacity in China in other ways as well, such as paying workers below the minimum wage or contravening food safety regulations. Indigenous Chinese companies have barely profited from this: Their repeated attempts to imitate foreign competitors have largely proved unsustainable. The same applies to development of alternative concepts that attempt to combine local tradition and mass production. Even massive government support and emphasis on the positive medicinal effects of these products have failed.

> My [Manchurian] forebears are said to have particularly liked cow's and mare's milk, and butter and cheese. But after living in Beijing for several generations, their traditional consumption of milk continually decreased. . . . Only my aunt sometimes drank a little milk, maybe just to prove she could afford it.
>
> *Zhenghongqi xia* (around 1965), chapter 7

The Coca-Cola China System

Coca-Cola is one of the most well-known international brands in China, with a leading position in the soft drinks market. Since re-entering China in 1979, Coca-Cola has invested more than US $5 billion in the local market, including US $3 billion investments from 2009 to 2011. By the end of March 2012, Coca-Cola has established a total of 42 bottling plants in China. Now the Coca-Cola system employs more than 50,000 people, virtually 99 per cent of which are local-hires. Coca-Cola and its bottlers have always been active corporate citizens in China, promoting sustainable environmental projects and development of local communities through education and cooperative public-private endeavors with a total contribution of over RMB 200 million in China. Coca-Cola is also the only corporation that has sponsored Special Olympics, Paralympic Games, EXPO and Universiade in China.

Coca-Cola Press Centre Press Kits, Pacific, March 29, 2012

What are the reasons? People in China are certainly interested in visiting McDonalds and Co. because of the unified standards of hygiene, the consistent quality of the food, and curiosity about Western lifestyles. There is, however, another important motivation. The advertising specifically targets the "little emperors," the children and young people who mostly grow up without siblings because of the restrictive population policy and who manage to persuade the family to give them nearly everything money can buy. The spoiling of the younger generation is not only creating a social paradigm change, but also aggravating a previously negligible health risk in China: overweight. Ironically, this is happening at the same time as excessive thinness is being idolized.

The U.S. fast food chains in China, which now include increasing numbers of Starbucks-type coffee shops, may boast impressive income growth, but they have not managed to displace the snack bars that have been providing light meals at least since the era of the Tang dynasty. They are in imminent danger, however, for it is small businesses that are most at risk in the center of the megacities. The threat comes less from competition of whatever kind than from the regulation mania of

Drive in? (advertisement, 2008)

government authorities that use deficient hygiene conditions as a welcome pretext for getting rid of cook-shops, stalls, and little outdoor restaurants.

Feeble Compromises

For many centuries the influence of Chinese culinary arts was mainly limited to the countries of East and Southeast Asia, where Confucian elites held power (such as Korea) or where large emigrant groups lived (the Malaysian peninsula, for example). Only a few things traveled further afield, such as the knowledge of how to make and cook noodles, which spread to Europe over the centuries. Of course, isolated examples of noodles were also found earlier in Europe, but it is hardly a coincidence that Italian pasta finally conquered the market at the time of intensive cultural transfer between Asia and Europe, initially through Arab mediation, and later through the spread of the vast Mongolian empire. Incidentally, there is no historical evidence whatsoever for the widespread assumption that the Venetian explorer Marco Polo (1251–1324), who is said to have lived in China for seven years, was personally responsible for bringing noodles to Europe.

Reverse feedback sometimes occurred, as when Yuan Mei, writing in chapter 12 of his classic cookbook *Suiyuan shidan*, which was completed in 1790, described eating excellent dumplings in Canton. Filled with meat and cooked by steaming, they were called *dianbuleng*. That is the only mention of this term, composed of three characters, in the literature, and its meaning is indecipherable, which indicates it could be a loan word. Following this thread brings us to the English word *dumpling*, which sounds similar and appears in almost every standard dictionary today as the translation for *jiao*, the term Yuan Mei used to explain what he had eaten. It is entirely possible that in Canton, a port frequented by British traders and sailors, a classic Chinese dish could be given a foreign name.

The region around Canton was also the starting point for a huge emigration movement that swept to the countries of Southeast Asia in the nineteenth century, and reached as far as the United States. Initially attracted by the Gold Rush in California, many of the emigrants (nearly 60 percent of whom came from Taishan district in the southeast of Canton), found jobs in coal pits, railway construction, agriculture, and

CHINESE POPULATION OF THE UNITED STATES (INCLUDING HAWAII FROM 1900 ON)

1850	1860	1870	1880	1890	1900	1910	1920
725	35,586	63,199	105,465	109,776	118,746	94,414	85,202

other occupational areas that required physical strength and stamina. Those who came to the cities, however, mostly worked in the service sector, crafts, and commerce. A list compiled in 1877 of the twenty-two most important jobs done by Chinese people in San Francisco included 7,500 cigar rollers, 5,000 traders, 4,500 domestic servants, and 3,500 laundry workers, whereas the numbers of kitchen staff, washers-up, and waiters seem to have been so small that they were not worth mentioning in the statistics.

In other words, Chinese immigrants initially cooked almost entirely for themselves. This only changed from 1882 on, when the legislators, urged on by the labor unions, began ousting immigrants from their jobs by imposing a series of new restrictions. The alternative, particularly in the big cities on the east and west coasts, was often to open a restaurant, and by 1920 there were 11,438 Chinese people working in the catering industry. But what happened to persuade the inhabitants of the United States, who were generally Sinophobic, to pay a visit to a Chinese restaurant, given the widespread suspicion that rats were cooked there? It was actually one key dish that triggered the boom: chop suey. Fortunately, the customers did not understand this term, which derives from the Cantonese *zaapseoi* (or *zasui* in Mandarin) and means "hodgepodge," which hardly sounds appetizing. In fact, it's very accurate, because the recipe calls for an optional amount of ingredients to be stir-fried or steamed, and then cooked in stock. There are only two other specifications: Everything should be chopped into small pieces, and soy sauce is always added.

This may not be original, but it does give plenty of scope for creativity. Every cook can add his or her own variations. Various, colorful legends exist about the origin of the dish, but they all support the claim that it was invented in the United States. Probably the most frequently cited story is that toward the end of the nineteenth century, a restaurant owner who had run out of supplies spontaneously served his hungry guests a reheated mixture of assorted leftovers, and when they asked enthusiastically what it was called, he replied, "chop suey." The setting of this legend is usually a simple eating-place in the "Wild West," or sometimes a posh East Coast establishment where the names of famous guests—such as the statesman Li Hongzhang, who dined at the Waldorf Astoria in 1896—are associated with this historic culinary birth.

That this dish and the story of its naming are not unknown in Tai-shan, the starting point for the emigration, has caused some historians to challenge tradition and argue that this was where it originated. That version is rather unconvincing, because all the evidence for it comes from a time when chop suey had already been popular in the United States for a long time. The answer is probably very simple. There were several waves of remigration back to China from the diaspora, and given the importance the Chinese place on communication within the family, it would be very surprising if news about the great culinary success story in the United States had not circulated back home to the old country.

There is absolutely no doubt about the origin of another purported Chinese specialty: fortune cookies. The crispy confections sweetened with sugar each contain a paper slip, usually printed with a rather simple proverb or motto, or sometimes a numerical combination that is supposed to help you win at the next lottery. A story still told today holds that David Jung, founder of the Hong Kong Noodle Company based in Los Angeles, invented the fortune cookie in 1918. This is doubtful, because Japanese immigrants have also been given the credit—probably rightly. At least, the few reliable sources always cited in the debate about the inventors make this version seem more plausible. Incidentally, Chinese restaurants in the United States not infrequently have a Japanese owner, and many Hispanics, especially Mexican immigrants, work in the kitchens. Moreover, this is a growing trend. Hispanics have long since made up the majority of the workforce in the factories that produce fortune cookies.

Three billion fortune cookies are manufactured annually worldwide, mostly in the United States; relatively few are made in China. After several bankruptcies, some Chinese firms are specializing in production again, but domestic demand is limited because the customers are so unfamiliar with the cakes that some firms feel obliged to market them with instructions for use. In any case, packaging costs regularly exceed

> (1) Open the packet; (2) Break open the fortune cookie using both hands; (3) Take out the slip of paper and read the proverb; (4) Eat the fortune cookie.
>
> Label on cookies from the company Beijing xingu qianyu (2008)

production costs, not least because the cookies are purchased in Beijing and Shanghai, mainly as gifts: to show affection or to celebrate a birth, a wedding, or passing examinations.

Another delicacy largely unknown in China, although it supposedly originated there, consists of chicken pieces covered in sticky sweet-and-sour sauce. Widely available in many variations, the recipe is named after Zuo Zongtang (1812–1885), a general not greatly renowned for his subtlety. It is impossible to find out exactly why "General Tso's chicken" has been hugely popular in the United States since the 1970s. This popularity may have been partly due to a TV cookery program, but that can hardly be the reason for the remarkable demand, and neither can the broccoli topping that people in the West (but only in the West) regard as typically Chinese. Although Zuo Zongtang apparently had no reputation as a gourmet, it is doubtful he would have been proud of his attributed sponsorship. His descendants are certainly very annoyed.

Some superb Chinese cooks in the West feel a bond with their home country's tradition and are capable of great creativity. Still, this hardly compensates for the miserable performance of many Chinese restaurants abroad. The lack of qualified staff is exacerbated by the tendency to adapt too readily to the tastes of the host country, and to take the easy way out. The inordinate length of the menu can often be explained by the simple fact that every major ingredient, from eggplant to pork to carp, is combined with every available sauce, regardless of any sense of flavor. But the days when restaurants monopolized Chinese food culture are long gone. The large variety of Asian food stores nowadays, at least in big cities, makes it possible to cook even unusual Chinese dishes at home. When shopping, however, you should bear in mind the relevant regulations about species protection, and take particular care to clean herbs, vegetables, and fruit thoroughly. Always remember that you can find a substitute for anything, and looking for fresh local alternatives is invariably better than using stale imported goods. Most of the people who insist on offering their guests scorpions as snacks are more concerned with testing bravado than trying to achieve authenticity.

Finding the right cooking equipment is not always easy. Most gas and induction cookers are not capable of reaching the maximum temperatures required (which require ratings of at least 5 kilowatts), especially for quick frying, and this is the absolute precondition for using the wok at its best. Otherwise it is little more than a quaint accessory or, in the case of the popular electric variety, a superfluous toy for the dining table. You can certainly get better results with a normal gas stove and a flat pan. Anyway, the choice of dishes can greatly influence your success: If you decide from the outset to concentrate on dishes that require steaming, poaching, boiling, baking, or frying, you can considerably reduce the need to reach high temperatures quickly.

If you are still looking for more in the realm of Chinese cooking, we can suggest two other options, depending on your budget: (a) You can book a flight to China, which may cost considerably less than a pound of sea cucumber or swallows' nests; or (b) you can try out a first-class restaurant closer to home, because some star cooks have discovered the merits of Asian foods and preparation methods, and are not shy of presenting imaginative treats such as "Spring rolls with exotic vinaigrette," "Chinese-style spare ribs," or "Warm chocolate praline with Sichuan pepper, mango, and dill."

Tables from Chapters 2–4

TABLE 1
SELECTED OIL SEEDS

Plant	Botanical name	Main fatty acid group
Cotton	*Gossypium arboreum*	Linoleic acid
Peanut	*Arachis hypogaea*	Oleic acid
Hemp	*Cannabis sativa*	Linolenic acid
Linseed	*Linum usitatissimum*	Linolenic acid
Shiso	*Perilla frutescens*	Linolenic acid
Rapeseed	*Brassica napus*	Erucic acid
Turnip	*Brassica rapa*	Erucic acid
Opium poppy	*Papaver somniferum*	Linoleic acid
Sesame	*Sesamum indicum*	Oleic acid
Soy	*Glycine max*	Linolenic acid
Sunflower	*Helianthus annuus*	Linoleic acid
Tea bush	*Camellia spp.*	Oleic acid

TABLE 2
SELECTED *ALLIUM* PLANTS

Chinese chives	*Allium ramosum*	Leek	*Allium porrum*
Rakkyo onion	*Allium chinense*	Shallot	*Allium ascalonicum*
Garlic chives	*Allium tuberosum*	Sand leek	*Allium scorodoprasum*
Scallions	*Allium fistulosum*	Chives	*Allium schoenoprasum*
Garlic	*Allium sativum*	Onion	*Allium cepa*

TABLE 3
HARVEST YIELDS 1980–2005 (IN THOUSANDS OF METRIC TONS)

	Apples	Pears	Citrus fruits	Bananas	Grapes
1980	2,363	1,466	713	61	110
1985	3,614	2,137	1,808	631	361
1990	4,319	2,353	4,855	1,456	859
1995	14,008	4,942	8,225	3,125	1,742
2000	20,431	8,412	8,783	4,941	3,282
2005	24,011	11,324	15,919	6,518	5,794

TABLE 4
SELECTED FRUITS

Apple	*Malus* spp.
Apricot	*Prunus armeniaca*
Banana	*Musa paradisiaca*
Cherry	*Prunus pseudocerasus*
Chinese plum	*Prunus salicina*
Coconut	*Cocos nucifera*
Fig	*Ficus carica*
Grape	*Vitis vinifera*
Grapefruit	*Citrus maxima*
Japanese apricot (ume)	*Prunus mume*
Jujube	*Ziziphus jujuba*
Japanese persimmon	*Diospyros kaki*
Kiwi	*Actinidia chinensis*
Kumquat	*Fortunella* spp.
Lemon	*Citrus limon*
Longan	*Euphoria longana*
Loquat (Japanese medlar)	*Eriobotrya japonica*
Lychee	*Litchi chinensis*
Mandarin	*Citrus reticulata*
Mango	*Mangifera indica*
Mulberry	*Morus alba, Morus nigra*
Orange	*Citrus sinensis*
Papaya	*Carica papaya*
Peach	*Prunus persica*
Pear	*Pyrus* spp.
Pineapple	*Ananas comosus*
Pomegranate	*Punica granatum*
Star fruit	*Averrhoa carambola*
Common melon	*Cucumis melo*
Watermelon	*Citrullus lanatus*

TABLE 5
MEAT MAMMALS

Domestic pig	*Sus scrofa domestica*
Sheep	*Ovis aries*
Cow	*Bos taurus domesticus*
Dog	*Canis lupus familiaris*
Horse	*Equus ferus caballus*
Donkey	*Equus asinus asinus*
Mule	*Crossbreed of E. ferus and E. asinus*
Elk	*Cervus elaphus*
Père David's deer	*Elaphurus davidianus*
Tiger	*Panthera tigris*
Leopard	*Panthera pardus*
Wild boar	*Sus scrofa*
Crested porcupine	*Hystrix cristata*
Camel	*Camelus bactrianus*
Bear	*Ursus spp.*
Goat	*Capra hircus*
Asian gazelle	*Procapra spp.*
Reeves muntjac	*Muntiacus reevesi*
Chinese water deer	*Hydropotes inermis*
Musk deer	*Moschus moschiferus*
Badger	*Meles meles*
Hare	*Lepus spp.,*
European rabbit	*Oryctolagus cuniculus*
Beaver	*Castor fiber*
Common otter	*Lutra lutra*
Asian elephant	*Elephas maximus*
Asiatic wild dog	*Cuon alpinus*
Wolf	*Canis lupus*
Red fox	*Vulpes vulpes*
Wildcat	*Felis silvestris*
Leopard cat	*Prionailurus bengalensis*
Domestic cat	*Felis silvestris catus*
Raccoon dog	*Nyctereutes procyonoides*
Wild horse	*Equus ferus przewalskii*
Rat	*Rattus spp., Rhizomys spp.*
Marmot	*Marmota spp.*
Marten	*Martes spp.*
Weasel	*Mustela spp.*
Hedgehog	*Erinaceus spp.*

From the *Yinshi xuzhi* (1350), chapter 8.

TABLE 6
BIRDS USED FOR NUTRITION

Whooper swan	*Cygnus cygnus*
Whistling swan	*Cygnus columbianus*
Mute swan	*Cygnus olor*
Swan goose	*Anser cygnoides*
Greater white-fronted goose	*Anser albifrons*
Bar-headed goose	*Anser indicus*
Siberian crane	*Grus leucogeranus*
Black-necked crane	*Grus nigricollis*
Common crane	*Grus grus*
Eurasian curlew	*Numenius arquata*
Chicken	*Gallus gallus domesticus*
Common pheasant	*Phasianus colchicus*
Hazel grouse	*Tetrastes bonasia*
Mallard	*Anas platyrhynchos*
Pintail	*Anas acuta*
Mandarin duck	*Aix galericulata*
Tufted duck	*Aythya fuligula*
Pigeon	Columba spp., *Streptopelia* spp.
Great bustard	*Otis tarda*
Collared crow	*Corvus torquatus*
Eurasian tree sparrow	*Passer montanus*
Bunting	*Emberiza* spp.

From the *Yinshan zhengyao* (1330), chapter 3.

TABLE 7
THE MAJOR FISH AND MOLLUSKS AT SHANGHAI'S MARKETS IN THE 1930S

English name	Zoological name	Average price per *jin* (approx. 600 g)
Common carp	*Cyprinus carpio*	24 fen
Black carp	*Mylopharyngodon aethiops*	20 fen
Grass carp	*Ctenopharyngodon idellus*	30 fen
Silver carp	*Hypophthalmichthys molitrix*	26 fen
Golden carp	*Carassius auratus*	20 fen
False salmon	*Elopichthys bambusa*	20 fen
Culter	*Culter brevicauda*	20 fen
Semiculter	*Hemiculter leucisculus*	15 fen
Bighead carp	*Aristichthys nobilis*	30 fen
Bream	*Parabramis bramula*	18 fen
Mandarin fish	*Siniperca chuatsi*	35 fen
Roach	*Squaliobarbus curriculus*	90 fen
Bullhead	*Odontobutis potamophila*	48 fen
Finless eel	*Fluta alba*	60 fen
Big yellow croaker	*Pseudosciaena amblyceps*	28 fen
Small croaker	*Pseudosciaena undovittata*	14 fen
Slate-cod croaker	*Cilus gilberti*	27 fen
Chinese croaker	*Nibea sina*	30 fen
Herring	*Ilisha elongata*	30 fen
Reeves' shad	*Tenualosa reevesii*	30 fen
Chinese mackerel	*Scomberomorus sinensis*	35 fen
Japanese saury	*Scomberomorus niphonius*	32 fen
Pomfret	*Stromateoides argentus*	20 fen
Sole	*Cynoglossus abbreviatus*	15 fen
Anchovy	*Coilia nasus*	20 fen
Sea bream	*Pagrosomus major*	30 fen
Sea bass	*Lateolabrax japonicus*	20 fen
Ice-fish	*Salanx chinensis*	15 fen
Mullet	*Mugil cephalus*	32 fen
Dogfish	*Squalus mitsukurii*	17 fen
Marine eel	*Muraenesox cinereus*	28 fen
Cuttlefish	*Sepiella japonica*	8 fen

Note: The hourly wage for textile workers at that time was between 3 and 12 fen.
Source: Reid 1939, with updated zoological names.

TABLE 8
SELECTED CULTIVATED PLANTS MENTIONED IN THE SIMIN YUELING
(AROUND 160)

Proso millet	*Panicum miliaceum*
Foxtail millet	*Setaria italica*
Barley	*Hordeum vulgare*
Rice	*Oryza sativa*
Taro	*Colocasia esculenta*
Yams	*Dioscorea polystachya*
Rice bean	*Vigna umbellata*
Azuki bean	*Vigna angularis*
Fava bean	*Vicia faba*
Soybean	*Glycine max*
Common melon	*Cucumis melo*
Bottle gourd	*Lagenaria siceraria*
Hemp	*Cannabis sativa*
Sesame	*Sesamum indicum*
Bok choy	*Brassica rapa*
Scallion	*Allium fistulosum*
Leek	*Allium porrum*
Garlic	*Allium sativum*
Water pepper	*Polygonum hydropiper*
Egoma	*Perilla frutescens*
Alfalfa	*Medicago sativa*
Ginger	*Zingiber officinale*
Mustard	*Brassica juncea*
Chinese mallow	*Malva verticillata*
Common cocklebur	*Xanthium strumarium*
Apricot	*Prunus armeniaca*
Peach	*Prunus persica*
Chinese plum	*Prunus salicina*
Jujube	*Ziziphus jujuba*
Chinese bitter orange	*Poncirus trifoliata*
Chinese lacquer tree	*Rhus verniciflua*
Mulberry tree	*Morus alba*
Tung tree	*Aleurites fordii*

TABLE 9
CHINA'S ETHNIC MINORITIES

Group	Main settlement area	Demographical data in 2000
Achang	Southwest (Yunnan)	33,936
Bai (Minjia)	Southwest (Yunnan)	1,858,063
Baoan	North (Gansu)	16,505
Benglong De'ang	Southwest (Yunnan)	17,935
Blang	Southwest (Yunnan)	91,882
Buyei (Bouyei)	Southwest (Guizhou)	2,971,460
Daur (Dagur, Dagour, Tahur)	North (inner Mongolia)	132,394
Dai	Southwest (Yunnan)	1,158,989
Dong (Kam)	Southwest (Guizhou)	2,960,293
Dongxiang (Santa)	North (Gansu)	513,805
Dulong (Drong, Drung, Deang)	Southwest (Yunnan)	7,426
Ewenki (Evenki, Owenki)	North (inner Mongolia)	30,505
Gaoshan (Kaoshan)	Southeast (Taiwan)	4,461
Gelao	Southwest (Guizhou)	579,357
Hani	Southwest (Yunnan)	1,439,673
Hezhen (Hezhe, Heche, Holchih)	Northeast (Heilongjiang)	4,640
Hui	North (Ningxia)	9,816,805
Jing (Gin, Vietnamese)	South (Guangxi)	22,517
Jingpo (Kachin)	Southwest (Yunnan)	132,143
Jino	Southwest (Yunnan)	20,899
Kazakh	Northwest (Xinjiang)	1,250,458
Kyrgyz (Kirghiz)	Northwest (Xinjiang)	160,823
Koreans	Northeast (Jilin)	1,923,842
Lahu	Southwest (Yunnan)	453,705
Li	South (Hainan)	1,247,814
Lisu	Southwest (Yunnan)	634,912
Lhoba (Lhopa, Lopa, Loyu)	West (Tibet)	2,965
Manchu (Manchurians)	Northeast (Liaoning)	10,682,262
Maonan	South (Guangxi)	107,166
Monba (Monpa, Moinba)	West (Tibet)	8,923
Miao (Hmong)	Southwest (Guizhou)	8,940,116
Mongols	North (inner Mongolia)	5,813,947
Mulao (Molao, Mulam)	South (Guangxi)	207,352
Naxi (Nahki, Moso)	Southwest (Yunnan)	308,839
Nu	Southwest (Yunnan)	28,759
Oroquen (Orochon, Olunchun, Elunchun)	North (inner Mongolia)	8,196
Pumi (Primi)	Southwest (Yunnan)	33,600
Qiang	Southwest (Sichuan)	306,072
Russians	Northwest (Xinjiang)	15,609
Salar	North (Qinghai)	104,503
She	Southwest (Fujian)	709,592

(continued)

TABLE 9 (*continued*)

Group	Main settlement area	Demographical data in 2000
Sui	Southwest (Guizhou)	406,902
Tajik	Northwest (Xinjiang)	41,028
Tatars	Northwest (Xinjiang)	4,890
Tibetan (Zang)	West (Tibet)	5,416,021
Tu (Monguor)	North (Qinghai)	241,198
Tujia	South (Hunan)	8,028,133
Uyghur	Northwest (Xinjiang)	8,399,393
Uzbek	Northwest (Xinjiang)	12,370
Va	Southwest (Yunnan)	396,610
Xibe (Sibo, Hsipo)	Northwest (Xinjiang)	188,824
Yao (Mien)	South (Guangxi)	2,637,421
Yi (Lolo)	Southwest (Sichuan)	7,762,272
Yugur (Yugu, Yuku, Yellow Uyghur)	North (Gansu)	13,719
Zhuang (Chuang, Tong)	South (Guangxi)	16,178,811

Bibliography

Western Sources and Further Reading

Anderson, Eugene N. "'Heating' and 'Cooling' Foods in Hong Kong and Taiwan," *Social Science Information* 19 (1980): 237–268.
——. *The Food of China*. New Haven: Yale University Press, 1988.
——. "Up Against Famine. Chinese Diet in the Early 20th Century," *Crossroads* 1 (1990): 11–24.
Ang, Andra. To the People, Food Is Heaven. *Stories of Food and Life in a Changing China*. Guilford, CT: Lyons Press, 2012.
Anusasananann, Linda Lau. *The Hakka Cookbook. Chinese Food Around the World*. Berkeley: University of California Press, 2012.
Barrow, John. *Travels in China*. Philadelphia: W. F. McLaughlin, 1805. New edition: Cambridge: Cambridge University Press, 2010. Download at http://www.manybooks.net/titles/barrows2872928729–8.html
Bauer, Wolfgang. "Die Nudeln des Marco Polo. Nachrichten vom chinesischen Kontinent des Geschmacks." In Uwe Schultz, ed. *Speisen, Schlemmen, Fasten. Eine Kulturgeschichte des Essens,* pp. 103–118. Frankfurt am Main, Leipzig: Insel, 1993.
Becker, Jasper. *Hungry Ghosts. China's Secret Famine*. New York: The Free Press, 1996.
Bodde, Derk. *Festivals in Classical China. New Year and Other Annual Observances During the Han Dynasty*. Princeton: Princeton University Press, 1975.
Boilleau, Gilles. "Conferring Meat in Archaic China. Between Reward and Humiliation," *Asiatische Studien* 40 (2006): 737–772.
Bokenkamp, Stephen R. *Early Daoist Scriptures*. Berkeley: University of California Press, 1997.
Bown, Tiffany. *Food and Drink in Han China*. (Dissertation). Cambridge, 1989.
Bray, Francesca. *Agriculture*. In Joseph Needham, ed. *Science and Civilisation in China*, Vol. 6.2. Cambridge: Cambridge University Press, 1984.
——. *The Rice Economies: Technology and Development in Asian Societies*. Cambridge: Cambridge University Press, 1986.
Bray, Tamara L., ed. *The Archaeology and Politics of Food and Feasting in Early States and Empires*. New York: Kluwer Academic/Plenum, 2003.
Brown, Lester R. *Who Will Feed China? Wake-Up Call for a Small Planet*. New York: W.W. Norton & Co., 1995.
Buck, John Lossing. *Chinese Farm Economy*. Chicago: University of Chicago Press, 1930.

Buell, Paul. D. and Eugene N. Anderson. *A Soup for the Qan. Chinese Dietary Medicine of the Mongol Era as Seen in Hu Szu-Hui's Yin-Shan Cheng-Yao*. London, New York: Kegan Paul/Columbia University Press, 2000.

Butz, Herbert. *Yüan Hung-tao's "Reglement beim Trinken" (Shang-cheng). Ein Beitrag zum essayistischen Schaffen eines Literatenbeamten der späten Ming-Zeit*. Frankfurt: Haag + Herchen, 1988.

Campany, Robert Ford. *To Live as Long as Heaven and Earth. A Translation and Study of Ge Hong's Traditions of Divine Transcendents*. Berkeley: University of California Press, 2002.

——. "The Meanings of Cuisines of Transcendence in Late Classical and Early Medieval China," *T'oung Pao* 91 (2005): 1–57.

Chang Kwang-chih, ed. *Food in Chinese Culture. Anthropological and Historical Perspectives*. New Haven: Yale University Press, 1977.

Chen Fangmei. *Shang Zhou qingtong jiuqi*. Taipei: Guoli Gugong bowuyuan, 1989.

Chen Feng. *Die Entdeckung des Westens. Chinas erste Botschafter in Europa 1866–1894*. Frankfurt: Fischer Taschenbuch, 2001.

Chen Guidi and Wu Chuntao. *Zur Lage der chinesischen Bauern*. Frankfurt: Zweitausendeins, 2011.

Chen Weiming. *Tang Song yinshi wenhua fazhanshi*. Taipei: Taiwan xuesheng shuju, 1995.

Chen Zhao. *Meishi xunqu. Zhongguo zhuanshi wenhua*. Shanghai: Guji chubanshe, 1991.

Cheng Qianfan. "One Sober and Eight Drunk. Du Fu's Song of the Eight Drunken Immortals," *Social Science in China* 4 (1985): 83–94.

Cheng Yisheng. *Anji wenwu jingcui*. Beijing: Wenwu chubanshe, 2003.

Cheung, Sidney C. H. and Tan Chee-Beng, eds. *Food and Foodways in Asia. Resource, Tradition and Cooking*. London, New York: Routledge, 2007.

Chitty, J. R. *Things Seen in China*. New York: E.P. Dutton & Co., 1909.

Cho, Lily. *Eating Chinese. Culture on the Menu in Small Town Canada*. Toronto: University of Toronto Press, 2010.

Chong, Key Ray. *Cannibalism in China*. Wakefield: Longwood Academic, 1990.

Chuan Han-sheng and Kraus, Richard A. *Mid-Ch'ing Rice Markets and Trade. An Essay in Price History*. Cambridge, MA: Harvard University Press, 1975.

Clunas, Craig. *Superfluous Things. Material Culture and Social Status in Early Modern China*. Urbana: Illinois University Press, 1991.

Coe, Andrew. *Chop Suey. A Cultural History of Chinese Food in the United States*. New York: Oxford University Press, 2009.

Cook, Constance A. "Scribes, Cooks, and Artisans: Breaking Zhou Tradition," *Early China* 20 (1995): 241–277.

Cotterell, Arthur and Cotterell, Yong Yap. *Die Kultur der chinesischen Küche*. Berne: Scherz, 1987.

Counihan, Caroll and Penny van Esterik. *Food and Culture. A Reader*. New York: Routledge, 1997.

Croll, Elisabeth J. *Food Supply in China and Nutritional Status of Children*. Geneva: UNICEF, 1986.

Davis, Deborah S., ed. *The Consumer Revolution in Urban China*. Berkeley: University of California Press, 2000.

Davis, Lucille. *Court Dishes of China. The Cuisine of the Ch'ing Dynasty*. Rutland, VT: C. E. Tuttle Co., 1966.

Der Ling [Yu Deling]. *Zwei Jahre am Hof von Peking*. Dresden, Leipzig: H. Minden, 1915.

Dikötter, Frank, Lars Peter Laamann, and Xun Zhou. Narcotic Culture: *A History of Drugs in China*. London: Hurst, 2004.

——. *Things Modern. Material Culture and Everyday Life in China*. Chicago: University of Chicago Press, 2007.

Dong Xinlin. "Von anständigen Kindern und fliegenden Kranichen. Wandmalereien in mongolenzeitlichen Gräbern Chinas," *Antike Welt* 1 (2004): 3–9.

Doolittle, Justus. *Social Life of the Chinese. A Daguerreotype of Daily Life in China*. New York: Harper & Bros., 1865.

Du Fuxiang and Guo Yunhui. *Famous Restaurants in China*. Beijing: China Tourism Publishing House, 1982.

Du Jinghua and Zhu Baikun. *Zhongguo jiu wenhua*. Beijing: Xinhua chubanshe, 1992.

Dunlop, Fuchsia. *Revolutionary Chinese Cookbook*. New York: W.W. Norton, 2007.

——. *Shark's Fin & Sichuan Pepper*. New York: W.W. Norton, 2008.

Eberhard, Wolfram. "Die chinesische Küche. Die Kochkunst des Herrn von Suiyüan," *Sinica* 15.1 (1940): 190–228.

——. *Chinese Festivals*. New York: H. Schuman, 1952.

Edgerton-Tarpley, Kathryn. *Tears from Iron. Cultural Responses to Famine in 19th Century China*. Berkeley: University of California Press, 2008.

Eijkhoff, Pieter. *Wine in China. Its History and Contemporary Developments*. Utrecht: Nederlands Wijngilde, 2000.

Emmerich, Reinhard. "Ein voller Becher Weins zur rechten Zeit. Anmerkungen zu Tangzeitlichen Weingedichten," *Minima Sinica* 1 (1998): 125–152.

Engelhardt, Ute. "Dietetics in Tang China and the First Extant Works of Materia Medica." In Elisabeth Hsu, ed. *Innovation in Chinese Medicine*, pp. 173–191. Cambridge, New York: Cambridge University Press, 2001.

Engelhardt, Ute and Carl-Hermann Hempen. *Chinesische Diätetik*. Munich: Elsevier, Urban & Fischer, 1997.

Engelhardt, Ute and Rainer Nögel. *Rezepte der chinesischen Diätetik*. Munich: Elsevier, Urban & Fischer, 2009.

Farquhar, Judith. "Eating Chinese Medicine," *Cultural Anthropology* 9 (1994): 471–497.

——. *Appetites. Food and Sex in Postsocialist China*. Durham, NC: Duke University Press, 2002.

Fishlen, Michael. "Wine, Poetry, and History. Du Mu's Pouring Alone in the Prefectural Residence," *T'oung Pao* 80 (1994): 260–297.

Flitsch, Mareile. "Westküche mit Eßstäbchen. Überlegungen zur sozial-technischen Wahrnehmung der Welt im modernen chinesischen Alltag." In Martina Siebert and Raimund Kolb, eds. *Über Himmel und Erde*, pp. 127–151. Wiesbaden: Harrassowitz, 2006.

Franke, Herbert. "A Note on Wine," *Zentralasiatische Studien* 8 (1974): 241–245.

——. "Feuerwasser im China der Yüanzeit. Eine Prosadichtung von Chu Te-jun." In Helwig Schmidt-Glintzer, ed. *Das andere China*, 209–235. Wiesbaden: Harrassowitz, 1995.

French, Paul and Matthew Crabbe. *Fat China. How Expanding Waistlines Are Changing a Nation*. London: Anthem Press, 2010.

Fricker, Ute. "Schein und Wirklichkeit. Zur altchinesischen Frauenideologie aus männlicher und weiblicher Sicht im geschichtlichen Wandel," *Mitteilungen der Gesellschaft für Natur- und Völkerkunde Ostasiens* 112 (Hamburg, 1988).

Garner, Jonathan. *The Rise of the Chinese Consumer. Theory and Evidence*. Hoboken, NJ: Wiley, 2005.

Gernet, Jacques. *Daily Life in China on the Eve of the Mongol Invasion 1250–1276*. Stanford: Stanford University Press, 1962.

Gimm, Martin. "Die Frustration des Gelehrten, kulinarisch betrachtet. Eine poetische Abhandlung zum Vegetarianismus eines Song-Eremiten," *Zeitschrift der Deutschen Morgenländischen Gesellschaft* 146.1 (1996): 156–172.

Godley, Michael. "Bacchus in the East. The Chinese Grape Wine Industry, 1892–1938," *Business History Review* 60.3 (1986): 383–409.

Goepper, Roger, ed. *Das alte China. Menschen und Götter im Reich der Mitte*. Munich: C. Bertelsmann, 1995.

Guo Weimin and Zhang Chunlun. "Yuanling Huxishan yihao Han mu fajue jianbao," *Wenwu* 1 (2003): 36–55.

Grew, Raymond. *Food in Global History*. Boulder, CO: Westview Press, 1999.

Gwinner, Thomas A. P., *Essen und Trinken. Die klassische Kochbuchliteratur Chinas*. Frankfurt am Main: Haag + Herchen, 1988.

Haar, Barend J. ter. "Buddhist-Inspired Options. Aspects of Lay Religious Life in the Lower Yangzi from 1100 until 1340," *T'oung Pao* 87 (2001): 92–152.

Hamilton, Roy W., ed. *The Art of Rice. Spirit and Sustenance in Asia*. Berkeley: University of California Press, 2003.

Han Bowen, ed. *Gansu sichou zhi lu wenming*. Beijing: Kexue chubanshe, 2008.

Harper, Donald. "Gastronomy in Ancient China," *Parabola* 9.4 (1984): 39–47.

——. *Early Chinese Medical Literature. The Mawangdui Medical Manuscripts*. London, New York: Kegan Paul / Columbia University Press, 1998.

Hayter-Menzies, Grant. *Imperial Masquerade. The Legend of Princess Der Ling*. Hong Kong: Hong Kong University Press, 2008.

Hebei sheng wenwu yanjiusuo, ed. *Xuanhua Liao mu*. Beijing: Wenwu chubanshe, 2001.

Heiss, Mary Lou and Robert J. Heiss. *The Story of Tea. A Cultural History and Drinking Guide*. Berkeley: Ten Speed Press, 2007.

Hevia, James L. *Cherishing Men from Afar. Qing Guest Ritual and the McCartney Embassy of 1793*. Durham: Duke University Press, 1995.

Hirsbrunner, Marco. "Chinas kapitalistische Wende als kannibalistischer Exzess," *Asiatische Studien* 40 (2006): 895–915.

Ho Chui-mei. "Food for an 18th Century Emperor. Qianlong and his Entourage," *Proceedings of the Denver Museum of Natural History* 15 (1998): 75–83.

Ho Ping-ti. "The Introduction of American Food Plants into China," *American Anthropologist* 57 (1955): 191–201.

Ho Shun-Yee. "The Significance of Musical Instruments and Food Utensils in Sacrifices of Ancient China," *Monumenta Serica* 51 (2003): 1–18.

Hohenegger, Beatrice. *Liquid Jade. The Story of Tea from East to West*. New York: St. Martin's Press, 2007.

Höllmann, Thomas O. "Die Stellung des Hundes im alten China." In Hermann Müller-Karpe, ed. *Zur frühen Mensch-Tier-Symbiose*, pp. 157–174. Munich: Beck, 1983.

——. "Reis im Bambusrohr und andere Gerichte der Tsou," *Chinablätter* 18 (1991): 274–277.

——. "Der gepökelte König oder Anthropophagie und Abschreckung." In Rolf Peter Sieferle and Helga Breuninger, eds. *Kulturen der Gewalt. Ritualisierung und Symbolisierung von Gewalt in der Geschichte,* pp. 108–122. Frankfurt: Campus, 1998.

——. *Das alte China. Eine Kulturgeschichte*. Munich: Beck, 2008.

Hsiao Kung-chuan. *Rural China. Imperial Control in the 19th Century*. Seattle: University of Washington Press, 1960.

Hu Derong and Zhang Renqing. *Jin Ping Mei yinshi pu*. Beijing: Jingji ribao chubanshe, 1995.

Hu Shanyuan. *Gu jin jiushi*. Shanghai: Shanghai shudian, 1987.

Hu Teh-wei. *Tobacco Control Policy Analysis in China. Economics and Health*. Hackensack, NJ, World Scientific, 2008.

Hu, William C. *The Chinese Mid-Autumn Festival. Foods and Folklore*. Ann Arbor, MI: Ars Ceramica, 1990.

——. *Chinese New Year. Facts and Folklore*. Ann Arbor, MI: Ars Ceramica, 1991.

Huang Hsing-tsung. *Fermentations and Food Science*. In Joseph Needham, ed. *History of Science and Civilisation in China*, Vol. 6.5. Cambridge: Cambridge University Press, 2000.

Huang Huibai. "Viticulture in China," *HortScience* 15.4 (1980): 461– 466.

Hung, Eva. "Dongpo's Miscellaneous Records," *Renditions* 33–34 (1990): 123–140.

Jartoux, Pierre. "A Letter of F. Jartoux, Missioner of the Society of Jesus, in China to F. de Fontenay, of the Same Society, Peking Aug. 20, 1704." In N.N., ed. *The Travels of Several Learned Missioners of the Society of Jesus into Diverse Parts of the Archipelago, India, China, and America*, pp. 198–214. London, 1714.

Jen Lin-Liu. Serve the People. *A Stir-Fried Journey Through China*. Boston: Mariner Books, 2009.

Jiao Nanfeng ed. *Han Yangling*. Chongqing: Chongqing chubanshe, 2001.

Johansen, Ulla. "Vergorene und destillierte Milchgetränke. Kulturintegrierte Drogen bei den mittel- und nordasiatischen Viehzüchtern." In Gisela Völger and Karin von Welck, eds. *Rausch und Realität. Drogen im Kulturvergleich*, Vol. 1, pp. 363–372. Reinbek: Rowohlt 1982.

Juang Je Tsun. *The Regional Dishes of Fukien*. Hong Kong: Wanli Book Company, 1998.

Jun Jing, ed. *Feeding China's Little Emperors. Food, Children, and Social Change*. Stanford: Stanford University Press, 2000.

Jung, John. *Chopsticks in the Land of Cotton. Lives of the Mississippi Delta Chinese Grocers*. Cypress, CA.: Yin & Yang Press, 2008.

——. *Sweet and Sour. Life in Chinese Family Restaurants*. Cypress, CA.: Yin & Yang Press, 2011.

Kallgren, Joyce K., ed. "Food, Famine, and the Chinese Society," *Journal of Asian Studies* 41.4 (1982): 685–801.

Kandel, Jochen. *Das chinesische Brevier vom weinseligen Leben. Heitere Gedichte, beschwingte Lieder und trunkene Balladen der großen Poeten aus dem Reich der Mitte*. Berne, Munich: Scherz, 1985.

Kastner, Joerg. *Chinese Nutrition Therapy. Dietetics in Traditional Chinese Medicine*. Stuttgart, New York: Thieme, 2007.

Keyes, John D., *Food for the Emperor. Recipes of Imperial China with a Dictionary of Chinese Cuisine*. San Francisco: Gramercy Publishing Co., 1963.

Kleeman, Terry F. *Great Perfection. Religion and Ethnicity in a Chinese Millennial Kingdom*. Honolulu: University of Hawaii Press, 1998.

Knechtges, David R. "A Literary Feast. Food in Early Chinese Literature," *Journal of the American Oriental Society* 106.1 (1986): 49–63.

——. "Gradually Entering the Realm of Delight. Food and Drink in Early Medieval China," *Journal of the American Oriental Society* 117.2 (1997): 229–239.

Kohn, Livia. "Daoist Monastic Discipline. Hygiene, Meals, and Etiquette," *T'oung Pao* 87 (2001): 153–193.

——. *Monastic Life in Medieval Daoism. A Cross-Cultural Perspective*. Honolulu: University of Hawaii Press, 2003.

Kolb, Raimund T. "'Weder Laut noch Gestank und der Dämon verschwindet.' Ein kleiner historischer Blick auf den brauchtümlichen Umgang mit Latrinengöttern und –dämonen in China." In Raimund T. Kolb and Martine Siebert, eds. *Über Himmel und Erde*, pp. 229–259. Wiesbaden: Harrassowitz, 2006.

Kölla, Brigitte. "Der Traum von Hua in der Östlichen Hauptstadt. Meng Yuanlaos Erinnerungen an die Hauptstadt der Song," *Schweizer Asiatische Studien* 24 (1996).

Koo, Linda Chih-ling. *The Nourishment of Life. Health in a Chinese Society.* Hong Kong: Commercial Press, 1982.

——. "The Use of Food to Treat and Prevent Disease in Chinese Culture," *Social Science and Medicine* 18 (1984): 757–766.

Kuhn, Dieter. *Die Song-Dynastie (960–1279). Eine neue Gesellschaft im Spiegel ihrer Kultur.* Weinheim: Acta Humaniora, 1987.

——, ed. *Chinas goldenes Zeitalter. Die Tang-Dynastie (618–907 n. Chr.) und das kulturelle Erbe der Seidenstraße.* Heidelberg: Edition Braus, 1993.

Kung, James Kaising. "Food and Agriculture in Post-Reform China," *Modern China* 18.1 (1992): 138–170.

Kupfer, Peter. "Pu-taojiu. Neuere Einblicke in die Kulturgeschichte des Traubenweins in China." In Marc Hermann and Christian Schwermann, eds. *Zurück zur Freude. Studien zur chinesischen Literatur und Lebenswelt und ihrer Rezeption in Ost und West,* pp. 589–624. Sankt Augustin, Nettetal: Steyler Verlag, 2007.

——, ed. *Wine in Chinese Culture. Historical, Literary, Social and Global Perspectives.* Berlin: LIT, 2010.

Kwong, Kylie. *China. Die 88 Köstlichkeiten.* Munich: Christian-Verlag, 2009.

Lai, T. C. [Lai Tien- Chang]. *Chinese Food for Thought.* Hong Kong: Hong Kong Book Centre, 1978.

——. *At the Chinese Table.* Hong Kong: Hong Kong Book Centre, 1984.

Landsberger, Stefan R. *Chinesische Propaganda. Kunst und Kitsch zwischen Revolution und Alltag.* Cologne: Dumont, 1995.

——. "Mao as the Kitchen God. Ritual Aspects of the Mao Cult During the Cultural Revolution." *China Information* 11.2–3 (1996): 196–211.

Laufer, Berthold. *Sino-Iranica.* Chicago: Field Museum of Natural History, 1919.

Law, Kenneth, Lee Cheng Meng and Max Zhang. *Authentic Recipes from China.* Hong Kong: Periplus, 2012.

Lee, Denin D. *The Night Banquet. A Chinese Scroll Through Time.* Seattle: University of Washington Press, 2010.

Lee, Jennifer. *The Fortune Cookie Chronicles. Adventures in the World of Chinese Food.* New York: Twelve, 2008.

Leong, Sam. *Sensations.* Singapore: Marshall Cavendish Cuisine, 2008.

Leppman, Elizabeth J. *Changing Rice Bowl. Economic Development and Diet in China.* Hong Kong: Hong Kong University Press, 2005.

Lewis, Mark E. *Sanctioned Violence in Early China.* Albany, NY: State University of New York Press, 1990.

Li Hong. *Der Duft meiner Heimat. Die wunderbaren Rezepte meiner chinesischen Familie.* Hildesheim: Gerstenberg, 2011.

Li Hu. *Han Tang yinshi wenhuashi.* Beijing: Beijing shifan daxue chubanshe, 1998.

Li, Lillian M. *Fighting Famine in North China. State, Market, and Environmental Decline, 1690s–1990s.* Stanford: Stanford University Press, 2007.

Li, Lillian M. and Dray-Novery, Alison. "Guarding Beijing's Food Security in the Qing Dynasty. State, Market, and Police," *Journal of Asian Studies* 58.4 (1999): 992–1032.

Li Shangyuan. *Zhongguo chuantong jieri qutan.* Jinan: Shandong youyi chubanshe, 1989.

Li Shaobing. *Minguo shiqi de xishi fengsu wenhua.* Beijing: Beijing shifan daxue chubanshe, 1994.

Liu, Warren K. *KFC in China. Secret Recipe for Success.* Hoboken, NJ: John Wiley, 2008.

Li Zhengping. *Zhongguo jiu wenhua.* Beijing shi: Wuzhou chuanbo chubanshe, 2010.

Liao Yan. *Food and Festivals of China*. Philadelphia: Mason Crest Publishers, 2006.

Lienert, Ursula. *Das Imperium der Han*. Cologne: Museum für Ostasiatische Kunst der Stadt Köln, 1980.

Lin Naishen. *Zhongguo gudai pengtiao he yinshi*. *Beijing Daxue Xuebao* 2 (1957): 131–144.

——. *Zhongguo yinshi wenhua*. Shanghai: Shanghai renmin chubanshe, 1989.

Lin Yutang, *My Country and My People*. New York: Reynal & Hitchcock, 1935.

Lin Zepu, ed. *Zhongguo canyin mingdian dadian*. Qingdao: Qingdao chubanshe, 1997.

——. *Zhongguo mingchu dadian*. Qingdao: Qingdao chubanshe, 1997.

Lin Zhengqiu and Xu Hairong and Chen Meiqing. *Zhongguo Songdai caidian gaishu*. Beijing: Zhongguo shipin chubanshe, 1989.

Liu Junru. *Chinese Food*. Cambridge: Cambridge University Press, 2011.

Liu Lingcan, ed. *Beijing minjian fengsu bai tu*. Beijing: Shumu wenxian chubanshe, 1982.

Liu Zhaorui. *Zhongguo gudai yincha yishu*. Taipei: Boyuan, 1989.

Lo, Eileen Yin-fei. *Mastering the Art of Chinese Cooking*. San Francisco: Chronicle Books, 2009.

Lo, Kenneth, ed. *Complete Encyclopedia of Chinese Cooking*. London: Treasure Press, 1985.

Lo, Vivienne and Penelope Barrett. "Cooking Up Fine Remedies. On the Culinary Aesthetic in a 16th Century Chinese Materia Medica." *Medical History* 49 (2005): 395–422.

Lou Yudong, ed. *Famensi kaogu fajue baogao*. Beijing: Wenwu chubanshe, 2007.

Löwenstein, Andreas. *Weinbau in China*. Duisburg: Saarbrücken-Scheidt : Dadder, 1991.

Lu, Henry C. *Chinese System of Food Cures*. Malaysia: Pelanduk Publications, 1989.

Ma Chengyuan and Yue Feng. *Silu kaogu zhenpin*. Shanghai: *Shanghai yiwen chubanshe*, 1998.

Ma Jing. *Beijing Culinary Guide*. Beijing: China Light Industry Publishing House, 2002.

MacGowan, John. *Sidelights on Chinese Life*. London: Paul, Trench, Trübner, 1907.

Mallory, Walter H. *China. Land of Famine*. New York: American Geographical Society, 1926.

Marks, Robert B. "Rice Prices, Food Supply, and Market Structure in 18th Century South China," *Late Imperial China* 12.2 (1991): 64–116.

Martin-Liao, Tienchi. "Frauenerziehung im Alten China. Eine Analyse der Frauenbücher," *Chinathemen* 22 (1984).

Mazumdar, Sucheta. *Sugar and Society in China. Peasants, Technology, and the World Market*. Cambridge, MA: Harvard University Asia Center, 1998.

McDermott, Joseph P. *State and Court Ritual in China*. Cambridge: Cambridge University Press, 1999.

McGovern, Patrick E. *Ancient Wine. The Search for the Origins of Viniculture*. Princeton: Princeton University Press, 2003.

——. *Uncorking the Past. The Quest for Wine, Beer, and Other Alcoholic Beverages*. Berkeley: University of California Press, 2009.

Meng T'ien-p'ei and Gamble, Sidney. *Prices, Wages and the Standard of Living in Peking 1900–1924*. Peking: Peking Express Press, 1926.

Mollier, Christine. "Les cuisines de Laozi et du Buddha," *Cahiers d'Extrême-Asie* 11 (1999–2000): 45–90.

Mowe, Rosalind, ed. *Südostasiatische Spezialitäten. Eine kulinarische Reise*. Cologne: Könemann, 1998.

Murck, Alfreda. "Golden Mangoes: The Life Cycle of a Cultural Revolution Symbol," *Archives of Asian Art* 57 (2007): 1–22.

Naquin, Susan: *Peking. Temples and City Life, 1400–1900*. Berkeley: University of California Press, 2000.

Navarra, Bruno. *China und die Chinesen*. Bremen: M. Nössler, 1901.

Needham, Joseph and Lu Gwei-Djen. *Hygiene and Preventive Medicine in Ancient China*. In Needham, Joseph, ed. *Clerks and Craftsmen in China and the West*, pp. 340– 378. Cambridge: Cambridge University Press, 1970.

Newman, Jacqueline M. and Ruth Linke. "Chinese Immigrant Food Habits. A Study of the Nature and Direction of Change," *Royal Society of Health Journal* 106.2 (1982): 268– 271.

Newman, Jacqueline M. "Fujian. The Province and Its Foods," *Flavour and Fortune* 6.2 (1999): 13–20.

——. *Food Culture in China*. Westport, CT: Greenwood Press, 2004.

Nie Fengqiao, ed. *Zhongguo pengren yuanliao dadian*. Qingdao: Qingdao chubanshe, 1998.

Peng Mingquan, ed. *Zhongguo yaoshan dadian*. Qingdao: Qingdao chubanshe, 2000.

Pettersson, Bengt. "Cannibalism in the Dynastic Histories," *Bulletin of the Museum of Far Eastern Antiquities* 71 (1999): 73–189.

Piazza, Alan, ed. *Food Consumption and Nutritional Status in the PRC*. Boulder, CO: Westview Press, 1986.

Pirazzoli-t'Serstevens, Michèle. *The Han Dynasty*. New York: Rizzoli, 1982.

——. "A Second-Century Kitchen Scene," *Food and Foodways* 1 (1985): 95–103.

——. "The Art of Dining in the Han Period. Food Vessels from Tomb 1 at Mawangdui," *Food and Foodways* 4 (1991): 209–219.

Polo, Marco. *Milione*. [Tuscan manuscript "Ottimo" from around 1300 A.D. in the Biblioteca Nazionale di Firenze] Edizione critica a cura di Valeria Bertolucci Pizzorusso. Milan: Adelphi, 1994.

Poo Mu-chou. "The Use and Abuse of Wine in Ancient China," *Journal of the Economic and Social History of the Orient* 42.2 (1999): 123–151.

Powers, Jo Marie, ed. *From Cathay to Canada. Chinese Food in Transition*. Toronto: Ontario Historical Society, 1998.

Qi Dongfang and Shen Qinyan, eds. *Huawu da Tang chun. Hejiacun yibao jingcui*. Beijing: Wenwu chubanshe, 2003.

Qiu Pangtong. *Zhongguo miandian shi*. Qingdao: Qingdao chubanshe, 2000.

——. *Zhongguo caiyao shi*. Qingdao: Qingdao chubanshe, 2001.

Read, Bernard E. *Common Food Fishes of Shanghai*. Shanghai: North China Branch of the Royal Asiatic Society, 1939.

——. *Famine Foods Listed in the Chiu Huang Ben Ts'ao*. Shanghai: Henry Lester Institute of Medical Research, 1946.

Ren Rixin. "Shandong Zhucheng Han mu huaxiangshi," *Wenwu* 10 (1981): 14–21.

Roberts, John A. G. *China to Chinatown. Chinese Food in the West*. London: Reaktion, 2002.

Rozman, Gilbert. *Population and Marketing Settlement in Ch'ing-China*. New York: Cambridge University Press, 1982.

Rubin, Lawrence C. *Food for Thought. Essays on Eating and Culture*. Jefferson, NC: McFarland, 2008.

Rubruk, Wiliam of. *Itinerarium fratris Willielmi de Rubruquis de ordine fratrum minorum, Galli, Anno gratia 1253 ad parte Orientales*. Reprinted and translated in Richard Hakluyt, ed. *The Principal Navigations, Voyages, Traffiques, and Discoveries of the English Nation*, Vol. 1. London, 1598.

Ruddle, Kenneth and Zhong Gongfu. *Integrated Agriculture—Aquaculture in South China. The Dike-Pond System of the Zhujiang Delta*. New York: Cambridge University Press, 1988.

Sabban, Françoise. "Court Cuisine in 14th Century Imperial China," *Food and Foodways* 1 (1986): 161–196.

——. "Ravioli cristallins et tagliatelle rouges. Les pâtes chinoises entre 12ᵉ et 14ᵉ siècle," *Médiévales* 16–17 (1989): 29–50.

——. "De la main à la pâte. Réflexion sur l'origine des pâtes alimentaires du blé en Chine ancienne," *L'homme* 30 (1990): 102–137.

——. "La viande en Chine. Imaginaire et les usages culinaires," *Anthropozoologica* 18 (1993): 79–90.

——. "La diète parfaite d'un lettre retiré sous les Song du Sud," *Études chinoises* 16.1 (1997): 1–51.

Schafer, Edward H. "The Development of Bathing Costumes in Ancient and Medieval China and the History of the Floriate Palace," *Journal of the American Oriental Society* 76.2 (1956): 57–82.

——. *The Golden Peaches of Samarkand. A Study of T'ang Exotics*. Berkeley: University of California Press, 1963.

Schlotter, Katrin and Elke Spielmanns-Rome. *Culinaria. China*. Potsdam: H.F. Ullmann, 2010.

Schmidt-Glintzer, Helwig. "Zum Thema Wein und Trunkenheit in der chinesischen Literatur," *Zeitschrift der Deutschen Morgenländischen Gesellschaft Suppl. 5* (1980): 362–374.

Serventi, Silvano and Françoise Sabban. *Pasta: The Story of a Universal Food*. New York: Columbia University Press, 2002.

Shao Qin: "Tempest Over Teapots. The Vilification of Teahouse Culture in Early Republican China," *Journal of Asian Studies* 57 (1998): 1009–1041.

Shaw Yu-ming, ed. *Traditional Chinese Culture in Taiwan. The Chinese Art of Food and Drink*. Taipei: Kwang Hwa Publishing Co., 1991.

Shen Congwen. *Zhongguo gudai fushi yanjiu*. Shanghai: Shanghai shuian, 1999.

Shinoda Osamu. *Chûgoku tabemono shi no kenkyo*. Tokyo: Haksaka shoho, 1978.

—— and Tanaka Seiichi, eds. *Chûgoku shokkei shosho*. Tokyo: Shoseki bunbutsu ryutsukai, 1972–1973.

Shriver, Alexis. *Canned-Goods Trade in the Far East*. Washington: Government Printing Office, 1915.

Siao, Eva. *China. Photographien 1949–1967*. Heidelberg: Edition Braus, 1996.

Simoons, Frederick J. *Food in China. A Cultural and Historical Inquiry*. Boca Raton, FL: CRC Press, 1991.

Skinner, G. William. "Vegetable Supply and Marketing in Chinese Cities," *China Quarterly* 76 (1978): 733–793.

——. "Rural Marketing in China. Repression and Revival," *China Quarterly* 103 (1985): 393–413.

Smil, Vaclav. *China's Past, China's Future. Energy, Food, Environment*. New York: Routledge, 2004.

Smith, Christopher. "(Over)Eating Success. The Health Consequences of the Restoration of Capitalism in Rural China," *Social Science and Medicine* 37.6 (1993): 761–770.

So, Yan-Kit. *Yan-kit's Classic Chinese Cookbook*. New York: Dorling Kindersley, 2006.

Solomon, Charmaine. *The Complete Asian Cookbook*. New York: McGraw-Hill, 1976.

Sterckx, Roel, ed. *Of Tripod and Palate. Food, Politics, and Religion in Traditional China*. New York: Palgrave Macmillan, 2005.

Sterckx, Roel. *Food, Sacrifice, and Sagehoood in Early China*. Cambridge: Cambridge University Press, 2011.

——. "Sages, Cooks, and Flavours in Warring States and Han China," *Monumenta Serica* 54 (2006): 1–47.

Strickmann, Michel. *Chinese Magical Medicine*. Stanford: Stanford University Press, 2002.

Su Tong. *Rice*. New York: W. Morrow & Co., 1995.

Swann, Nancy Lee. *Food and Money in Ancient China*. Princeton: Princeton University Press, 1950.

Tan Chanxue, ed. *Dunhuang shiku quanji. Minsu hua juan*. Hong Kong: Shang wu yin shu guan, 1999.

Tan, Sylvia. *Modern Nyonya*. Singapore: Marshall Cavendish International Asia, 2011.

Tan, Terry. *The Food and Cooking of Sichuan and West China*. Leicester: Anness, 2012.

Tang Sunlun. *Zhongguo chi*. Taipei: Dadi chubanshe, 2000.

Tao L. K. [Tao Menghe]: *Livelihood in Peking. An Analysis of the Budgets of Sixty Families*. Beijing: Social Research Dept., China Foundation for the Promotion of Education and Culture, 1928.

Tao Zhengang and Zhang Lianming, eds. *Zhongguo pengren wenxian tiyao*. Beijing: Zhongguo shangye chubanshe, 1986.

Teiwes, Frederick C. and Warren Sun. *China's Road to Disaster. Mao, Central Politicians, and Provincial Leaders in the Unfolding of the Great Leap Forward*. Armonk, NY: Sharpe, 1999. Also available as e-book.

Terrill, Ross. "Die Tore der Hölle öffneten sich weit," *Die Zeit* 23 (1996): 38.

Thaxton, Ralph A. Jr., *Catastrophe and Contention in Rural China. Mao's Great Leap Forward Famine and the Origins of Righteous Resistance in Da Fo Village*. New York: Cambridge University Press, 2008.

Trauffer, Regula. *Manger en Chine—Essen in China*. Vevey: Alimentarium, 1997.

Trombert, Eric. "Bière et Bouddhisme. La consommation de boissons alcoolisées dans les monastères de Dunhuang aux VIII^c–X^c siècles," *Cahiers d'Extrême-Asie* 11 (1999–2000): 129–181.

Trombert, Eric. "Cooking, Dyeing, and Worship. The Use of Safflower in Medieval China as Reflected in Dunhuang," *Asia Major* 3rd ser. 17.1 (2004): 59–72.

Unschuld, Paul Ulrich. *Pen-ts'ao. 2000 Jahre traditionelle pharmazeutische Literatur Chinas*. Munich: H. Moos, 1973.

Unschuld, Paul Ulrich. *Medicine in China: A History of Pharmaceutics*. Berkeley: University of California Press, 1986.

Wagner, Christoph and Peter Frese. *Garküchen. Vom Essen auf den Straßen und Märkten zwischen Peking und Hongkong*. Cologne: Komet, 2002.

Waley-Cohen, Joanna. *The Quest for Perfect Balance. Taste and Gastronomy in Imperial China*. In Paul H. Freedman, ed. *Food. The History of Taste*, pp. 99–134. Berkeley: University of California Press, 2007.

Wan Guoguang. *Zhongguo de jiu*. Beijing: Renmin chubanshe, 1986.

Wang Congren. *Zhongguo cha wenhua*. Shanghai: Shanghai wenhua chubanshe, 1991.

Wang Hu. *Zhongguo chuantong qiju sheji yanjiu*. Nanjing: Wenwu chubanshe, 2007.

Wang Juling. *Famous Dishes of Famous Restaurants in Beijing*. Beijing: Golden Shield Publishing House, 2000.

Wang Mingde and Wang Zihui. *Zhongguo gudai yinshi*. Xi'an: Shanxi renmin chubanshe, 1988.

Wang Renbo, ed. *Qin Han wenhua*. Shanghai: Shanghai keji jiaoyu chubanshe, 2001.

Wang Renxiang. *Yinshi yu zhongguo wenhua*. Beijing: Renmin chubanshe, 1994.

——. *Zhongguo yinshi tangu*. Beijing: Qinggongye chubanshe, 1985.

——. *Zhongguo gudai mingcai*. Beijing: Zhongguo shiping chubanshe, 1987.

——, ed. *Zhongguo shiqian yinshi shi*. Qingdao: Qingdao chubanshe, 1997.

——, ed. *Min yi shi wei tian. Zhongguo yinshi wenhua*. Jinan: Jinan chubanshe, 2004.

Wang Shouguo. *Jiu wenhua zhong de Zhongguoren*. Zhengzhou: Henan renmin chubanshe, 1990.

Wang Xiaoping and Benjamin Caballero. *Obesity and Its Related Diseases in China*. Youngstown, NY: Cambria Press, 2007.

Wang Xuetai. *Zhongguoren de yinshi shijie*. Hong Kong: Zhonghua shuju, 1989.

———. *Huaxia yinshi wenhua*. Beijing: Zhonghua shuju, 1993.

Wang Yeh-chien. "Food Supply in 18th-Century Fukien," *Late Imperial China* 7.2 (1986): 80–117.

Wang Zihui, ed. *Zhongguo caiyao dadian*. Qingdao: Qingdao chubanshe, 1995–1997.

Wang Zili and Sun Fuxi. *Tang Jinxiang xianzhu mu*. Beijing: Wenwu chubanshe, 2002.

Wang-Toutain, Françoise. "Pas de boissons alcoolisées, pas de viande. Une particularité du bouddhisme chinois vue à travers les manuscrits de Dunhuang," *Cahiers d'Extrême-Asie* 11 (1999–2000): 91–128.

Watson, James L. "From the Common Pot. Feasting with Equals in Chinese Society," *Anthropos* 82 (1987); 389–401.

———. *Golden Arches East. McDonalds in Asia*. Stanford: Stanford University Press, 1997.

Wegener, Georg. *Im innersten China. Eine Forschungsreise durch die Provinz Kiangsi*. Berlin: A. Scherl, 1926.

Weng, Weijian. *Zhongguo yinshi liaofa—Chinese Food Therapy*. Hong Kong: Yinshi tiandi chubanshe, 1991.

Weng Xiaoping and Benjamin Caballero. *Obesity and Related Diseases in China. The Impact of the Nutrition Transition in Urban und Rural Adults*. Amherst, NY: Cambria Press.

West, Stephen H. "Cilia, Scale and Bristle. The Consumption of Fish and Shellfish in the Eastern Capital of the Northern Song," *Harvard Journal of Asiatic Studies* 47.2 (1987): 595–634.

———. "Playing with Food. Performance, Food, and the Aesthetics of Artificiality in the Sung and Yuan." *Harvard Journal of Asiatic Studies* 57.1 (1997): 67–106.

Wilhelm, Richard. "Eine chinesische Speisekarte aus der Dschou-Dynastie," *Sinica* 5.1 (1930): 40–43.

Wilkinson, Endymion. "Chinese Culinary History," *China Review International* 8.2 (2001): 285–304.

Will, Pierre-Étienne. *Bureaucracy and Famine in 18th Century China*. Stanford: Stanford University Press, 1990.

——— and R. Bin Wong, eds. *Nourish the People. The State Civilian Granary System in China 1650–1850*. Ann Arbor, MI: Center for Chinese Studies, University of Michigan, 1991.

Williams, S. Wells. *The Middle Kingdom. A Survey of the Geography, Government, Literature, Social Life, Arts and History of the Chinese Empire and Its Inhabitants*. New York, 1883.

Wittwer, Sylvan et al. *Feeding a Billion. Frontiers of Chinese Agriculture*. East Lansing: Michigan State University Press, 1987.

Wu, David Y. H. and Sidney C. H. Cheung, ed. *The Globalization of Chinese Food*. Honolulu: University of Hawaii Press, 2002.

Wu, David Y. H. and Chee-beng Tan, ed. *Changing Chinese Foodways in Asia*. Hong Kong: Chinese University Press, 2001.

Wu Guoguang. *Zhongguo de jiu*. Taipei: Shuxin chubanshe, 1987.

Wu Hui. *Zhongguo lidai liangshi muchan yanjiu*. Beijing: Nongye chubanshe, 1985.

Wu Qianjun et al. "Investigation into Benzene, Trihalomethanes and Formaldehyde in Chinese Lager Beers," *Journal of the Institute of Brewing* 112.4 (2006): 291–294.

Xiao Fan, ed. *Zhongguo pengren cidian*. Beijing: Zhongguo shangye chubanshe, 1992.

Xiong Sizhi, ed. *Zhongguo yinshi shiwen dadian*. Qingdao: Qingdao chubanshe, 1995.

Xu Hairong, ed. *Zhongguo yinshi shi*. Beijing: Huaxia chubanshe, 1999.

Xu Ruqi, ed. *Food and Chinese Culture. Essays on Popular Cuisines*. San Francisco: Long River Press, 2005.

Xue Liyong: *Shisu quhua*. Shanghai: Shanghai kexue jishu wenxian chubanshe, 2003.

Yang Guotong and Ma Liyan. *Qingzhen caipu*. Beijing: Jindun chubanshe, 1992.

Yang, L. Dali. *Calamity and Reform in China. State, Rural Society, and Institutional Change Since the Great Leap Forward*. Stanford: Stanford University Press 1996.

Yates, Robin D. S. *War, Food Shortages, and Relief Measures in Early China*. In Lucile F. Newman and William C. Crossgrove, eds. *Hunger in History. Food Shortage, Poverty, and Deprivation*, pp. 147–177. Cambridge, MA: Blackwell, 1990.

Yee, Elaine et al., ed. *China Abroad. Travels, Subjects, Spaces*. Hong Kong: Hong Kong University Press, 2009.

Yin Shenping and Han Wei. *Tang mu bihua jijin*. Xi'an: Shanxi renmin meishu chubanshe, 1991.

Ying Yimin. *Putao meijiu yeguang bei*. Xi'an: Shaanxi renmin chubanshe, 1999.

Young, Grace. *The Breath of a Wok. Unlocking the Spirit of Chinese Wok Cooking Through Recipes and Lore*. New York: Simon and Schuster, 2004.

Yu Hui. *Jin Tang liang Song huihua. Renwu fengsu*. Hong Kong: Shangwu yinshu guan, 2005.

Yu Weichao, ed. *Huaxia zhi lu*. Beijing: Chaohua chubanshe, 1997.

Yuan Hongqi. *Zhongguo de gongting yinshi*. Beijing: Shangwu yinshu guan, 1997.

Yue Gang. *The Mouth that Begs. Hunger, Cannibalism, and the Politics of Eating in Modern China*. Durham, NC: Duke University Press, 1999.

Zeng Zongye. *Zhongguo mingjiu zhi*. Beijing: Zhongguo lüyou chubanshe, 1980.

Zhang Boxi, ed. *Jiayuguan Jiuquan Wei Jin Shiliuguo mubihua*. Lanzhou: Gansu renmin meishu chubanshe, 2001.

Zhang Junke. "Weinanbau in China. Vergangenheit, Gegenwart, Zukunft," *Gauweilerhof aktuell* 35.1 (2007): 20–27.

Zhang Menglun. *Han Wei yinshikao*. Lanzhou: Lanzhou daxue chubanshe, 1988.

Zhang Zheyong and Chen Jinlin and Gu Bingquan. *Yinshi wenhua cidian*. Changsha: Hunan chubanshe, 1993.

Zhao Rongguang. *Zhongguo yinshi wenhua shi*. Shanghai: Shanghai renmin chubanshe, 2006.

Zhao Shuangzhan and Zhao Linjuan. "Zhongguo gudai jianya yu yashua fazhan," *Wenbo* 3 (2005): 84–88.

Zheng Jinsheng. "The Vogue for 'Medicine as Food' in the Song Period," *Asian Medicine* 2 (2006): 38–58.

Zheng Yi. *Scarlet Memorial. Tales of Cannibalism in Modern China*. Boulder, CO: Westview Press, 1996.

Zhongguo lishi bowuguan and Xinjiang Weiwu'er zizhiqu wenwuju. *Tianshan gudao dong xi feng. Xinjiang sichou zhi lu wenwu teji*. Beijing: Zhongguo shehui kexue chubanshe, 2002.

Zhou Guangwu. *Zhongguo pengrenshi jianbian*. Guangzhou: Kexue puji chubanshe, 1984.

Zhou Sanjin. *Mingcai xiaoshi*. Shanghai: Xuelin chubanshe, 1986.

Zhu Shijin and Zhe Fuchang and Guan Zhiyuan. *Sanchu mingyao*. Beijing: Zhongguo shipin chubanshe, 1988.

Zhu Zhenfan. *Shilin waishi*. Taipei: Maitian chubanshe, 2002.

Zou Han. *Heilongjiang Hegang diqu gudai wenhua yicun*. Harbin: Heilongjiang renmin chubanshe, 2006.

Chinese and Japanese Sources Cited in This Book
(listed alphabetically by title)

Ba Wangshi huayanjing jie. Written by Su Shi in 1075, published in *Su Shi wenji*, Vol. 5, (Beijing 1986), p. 2060.

Baopuzi neipian. Written by Ge Hong around 320.

Beiji qianjin yaofang. Written by Sun Simiao in 652.

Beishan jiujing. Written by Zhu Gong around 1117.

Benxinzhai shushipu. Written by Chen Dasou around 1250.

Caochuang yunyu. Written by Zhou Mi in 1274.

Chaguan. Written by Lao She in 1957.

Chajing. Written by Lu Yu in 760.

Chaju tuzan. Compiled in 1269 by an unknown author under the pseudonym Shen'an laoren.

Chalu. Written by Cai Xiang in 1051.

Daguan chalun. Written by Emperor Huizong in 1107.

Dongjing meng Hua lu. Written by Meng Yuanlao in 1148.

Dongpo zhilin. Written by Su Shi in 1101 and published posthumously.

Ershinian mudu zhi gui xianzhuang. Written by Wu Woyao from 1906 to 1910.

Fayuan zhulin. Written by Dao Shi in 668.

Foguoji. Written by Faxian around 420.

Gengzhitu. Presented to the emperor by Lou Shou in 1145.

Gusu fanhua tu. Horizontal scroll, painted by Xu Yang in 1759.

Guanglusi zeli. 1839, compilers unknown.

Guanzi. Compiled by Liu Xiang in 26 B.C.

Guitianlu. Written by Ouyang Xiu in 1067.

Han Xizai yeyan tu. Horizontal scroll, painted by Gu Hongzhong around 960.

Hanshu. Compiled up to around 115 by Ban Biao, Ban Gu, and Ban Zhao.

Huaian fuzhi. Compiled by Chen Wenzhu in 1573.

Hunan nongmin yundong kaocha baogao. Report written by Mao Zedong in 1927. Published in *Mao Zedong xuanji* (Beijing 1951), Vol. 1, pp. 12–44.

Jiali. Written by Zhu Xi around 1190.

Jianzhi bian. Written by Yao Shilin in 1623.

Jiatai Kuaiji zhi. Compiled by Shi Su in 1201.

Jiayou ji. Written by Su Xun in 1055.

Jie yao. Written by Bo Juyi in 843. Poem, published in *Bo Xiangshan ji* (Shanghai 1933), Vol. 10, p. 77.

Jilei bian. Written by Zhuang Chuo in 1133.

Jin Ping Mei. Written by an anonymous author at the end of the sixteenth century; first printed in 1617.

Jiu Wudaishi. Compiled by Xue Juzheng in 974.

Jiuhuang bencao. Compiled by Zhu Su in 1406.

Jiujing. Written by Su Shi in 1090.

Jujia biyong shilei quanji. Compiled by an unknown author in the first half of the fourteenth century.

Laozi (or Daodejing). Attributed to Lao Dan (7th–6th century B.C.), but the core text was probably not compiled before the fourth century A.D.

Liaoshi. Compiled by Tuo Tuo in 1344.

Liji. Attributed to Dai Sheng (1st–2nd century), but probably only compiled towards the end of the second century.

Liu Mengde ji. Written by Liu Yuxi in 808.

Lunheng. Compiled around 75 A.D. from texts by Wang Chong (1st century).

Lunyu. Attributed to Confucius (6th–5th century B.C.) but probably only compiled around 450 B.C.; revised and expanded in second century B.C.

Lushan huiyi shilu. Written by Li Rui in 1989. Beijing.

Lüshi chunqiu. Attributed to Lü Buwei (3rd century B.C.); compiled around 240 B.C.

Meishijia. Compiled by Lu Wen-fu in 1983. *Shouhuo* 39.1, pp. 4–45.

Mengzi. Attributed to Meng Ke (4th–3rd century B.C.), but only compiled towards the end of the second century.

Min yi he shi wei tian? Zhongguo shipin anquan xianzhuang diaocha. Compiled by Zhou Qing in 2004, and republished in Beijing in 2007 after the ban.

Nittō guhō junrei kōki. Diary kept by Jikaku Daishi (Ennin) from 838–847.

Nongshu. Written by Chen Fu in 1149.

Nongshu. Written by Wang Zhen in 1313.

Nongsang jiayao. Compiled by Meng Qi (?) in 1273.

Nongsang yishi cuoyao. Written by Lu Mingshan in 1314.

Nongzheng quanshu. Written by Xu Guangqi in 1628.

Nü lunyu. Written by Song Ruoxin and Song Ruozhao around 780.

Qimin yaoshu. Compiled by Jia Sixie around 540.

Qiuranke zhuan. Probably written by Du Guangting around 900. Story, published in Ch. 193 of *Taiping guangji*, compiled by Li Fang in 981.

Sancai tuhui. Compiled by Wang Qi in 1609.

Shangzheng. Written by Yuan Hongdao in 1606.

Shanjia qinggong. Written by Lin Hong in the second half of the thirteenth century.

Shanzaixing. Poem written by Cao Pi around 210. Published in Ch. 27 of *Wenxuan*, compiled by Xiao Tong in 531.

Shengjitu. Unknown author, first printed in 1544.

Shiji. Compiled by Sima Qian in 81 B.C.

Shijing. Anonymous anthology of song texts, some supposedly dating back to the tenth century B.C., but the majority probably from the eighth century B.C.

Shinzoku kibun. Written by Nakagawa Tadahide in 1799.

Shipu. Compiled around 709; attributed to Wei Juyuan.

Shixian hongmi. Attributed to Wang Shizhen, but probably written by Zhu Yizun in 1680.

Shoushi tongkao. Compiled by E'ertai in 1742.

Shu Donggaozi zhuan hou. Colophon written by Su Shi in 1096. Published in *Su Shi quanji* (Beijing 2000), Vol. 3., p. 2086.

Simin yueling. Written by Cui Shi around 160.

Suiyuan shidan. Written by Yuan Mei in 1790.

Taiping yulan. Compiled by Li Fang in 983.

Taiwei lingshu ziwen xianji zhenji shangjing. Written by Yang Xi around 370.

Tangchao minghua lu. Written by Zhu Jingxuan around 845.

Tanglü shuyi. Compiled by Changsun Wuji et al.; became effective in 653.

Tiangong kaiwu. Written by Song Yingxing in 1637.

Tiaoding ji. Attributed to Tong Yuejian. Written around 1765 with subsequent additions.

Wanghuailu. Written by Shen Gua around 1070.

Wode qianban sheng. Written by Puyi in 1964 (with major collaboration by Li Wenda).

Wu niu tu. Horizontal scroll, painted by Han Huang around 770.

Wulei xianggan zhi. Attributed to Su Shi (11th–12th century), but probably written by Lu Zangning around 980.

Wulin jiushi. Written by Zhou Mi in 1270.

Wushi zhongkuilu. Probably compiled in the first half of the thirteenth century by a "Mrs. Wu" whose first name remains unknown.

Wu zazu. Compiled by Xie Zhaozhi in 1602.

Xianqing ouji. Written by Li Yu in 1671.

Xin shitou ji. Written by Wu Woyao in 1905.

Xing lu nan. Poem cycle written by Li Bo in 744. Published in *Li Taibo quanji* (Beijing 1977), Vol. 1, pp. 189–193.

Xu zizhi tongjian changbian. Compiled by Li Dao in 1072.

Xuanmen shishi weiyi. Written by an unknown author around the mid-seventh century.

Yalaji jiu fu. Prose poem written by Zhu Derun in 1344. Published in chapter 3 of *Cunfuzhai wenji* (Taipei 1966).

Yang xiaolu. Written by Gu Zhong in 1698.

Yanguan dabeige ji. Essay written by Su Shi in 1075. Published in *Su Shi wenji* (Beijing 1986) Vol. 2, pp. 386–387.

Yangzhou huafang lu. Written by Li Dou in 1795.

Yi Ya yiyi. Written by Han Yi in the first half of the fourteenth century.

Yin jiu ershi shou. Poem cycle written by Tao Yuanming in 403. Published in *Tao Yuanming ji* (Beijing 1979), pp. 86–100.

Yinshan zhengyao. Written by Hu Sihui in 1330.

Yinshi xuzhi. Compiled by Jia Ming in 1350.

Yinzhong baxian ge. Poem written by Du Fu in 746. Published in *Du shi xiangzhu* (Beijing 1979), Vol. 1, pp. 81–85.

Yinzhiwen tushuo. Compiled by Ya Zhang in 1801.

Yinzhuan fushi jian. Written by Gao Lian in 1591.

You yu Wei Chu qi Dayi ciwan. Poem written by Du Fu in 756. Published in Du Shaoling ji xiangzhu (Shanghai 1930), Vol. 4, p. 107.

Yu jian zashu. Written by Ye Mengde in the eleventh century.

Yuexia duzhuo. Poem, probably written in 744 by Li Bo. Published in *Li Taibo quanji* (Beijing 1977), Vol. 2, p. 1062.

Yunlintang yinshi zhidu ji. Written by Ni Zan in 1360.

Zhao qun chen. Edict written by Cao Pi (Emperor Wen of the Wei Dynasty) in 223. Published in *Quan Sandai Qin Han Sanguo Liuchao wen* (Beijing 1959), Vol. 2, p. 1082.

Zhaohun. Poem attributed to Qu Yuan (4th-3rd century B.C.). Published in *Chuci*, compiled by Wang Yi in 125.

Zhenghongqi xia. Autobiographical fragment by Lao She, written between 1960 and 1966, and published posthumously in 1979.

Zhenglun. Written by Cui Shi around 150.

"*Zhongguo de shipin anquan konghuang*." Written by Zhou Qing. *Zhongwai duihua* of 14.09.2006.

Zhouli. Compiled by Liu Xin at the beginning of the first century A.D. on the basis of older versions.

Zhuangzi. Attributed to Zhuang Zhou (4th-3rd century B.C.), revised and expanded later.

Zhufanzhi. Written by Zhao Rugua around 1225.

Zhulo xianzhi. Written by Chen Menglin around 1716.

Zoubi xie Meng jianyi ji xin cha. Poem written by Lu Tong around 835. Published in *Yuchuanzi shiji* (Taipei 1967), p. 8.

Zui zeng Zhang mishu. Poem written by Han Yu in 806. Published in *Han Changli shi xinian jishi* (Taipei 1966), pp. 177–180.

Zuixiang riyue. Written by He Manzi in 1991. Shanghai.

Index

Note: Page numbers in italics refer to illustrations and captions; those in bold-face refer to text boxes; a page number followed by *t* refers to a table.